BUSINESS CYCLE INDICATORS AND MEASURES

A Complete Guide to Interpreting the Key Economic Indicators

George Hildebrand

PROBUS PUBLISHING COMPANY
Chicago, Illinois
Cambridge, England

ISBN 1-55738-410-X

Printed in the United States of America

BB

1 2 3 4 5 6 7 8 9 0

CONTENTS

PREFACE

What started out as curiosity turned into a quest.

Indicators are quoted frequently in the news and on television. Bond and stock prices, political action, optimism or pessimism seem to all be affected by the announcement of the status of particular indicators.

An increased interest in predictive models started an inquiry to find out what indicators were, who they were developed by, why they were developed, where they have applicability, and how they are used.

The investigation seemed simple enough, but on getting involved, it became apparent that the desired information was scattered among many different publications. Needed explanatory or basic publications were out of print. Much of the information was only available on microfiche. The constant back-and-forth between the current and noncurrent publications reminded me of a rat trying to get out of a maze. This can be very discouraging to anyone desiring semi-immediate information.

The demise of the monthly government publication *Business Conditions Digest* in March 1990 because of budget and personnel constraints created a big question about how easy access to information would be in the future. Since the information was not that easily available in the past, it was reasonable to assume that easy future access may not be available to students and professionals.

The purpose of this handbook is to simplify an inquiry into business-cycle indicators by making an organized search for relevant information a less painful process.

Where possible, all of the definitions, the titles, and much of the text are as reported by the Bureau of Economic Analysis, Department of Commerce publications. References are cited for an easier source of additional material.

George H. Hildebrand

ACKNOWLEDGEMENTS

Many thanks are due to my student assistants, Anne Olmstead and Pui-lam Kwok. Sandra Lui put in some long hours getting the final draft ready for publication. My friend Meiwen Wu was especially helpful in constucting the charts and tables, with editing undertaken by my daughter, Linda. Their help with the data entry, word processing, editing and analysis contributed greatly to the completion of this book.

Assistance and suggestions were received from many parties. David Lilien of Quantitative Micro Software advised as to many of the procedures for the use of Micro TSP in graphing time-series data. Information about sources, possible uses of the book, and some background on the National Bureau of Economic Research was supplied by Donna Zerwitz of that organization.

Thanks are also due to Eunice Blue, Barry Beckman, and Mary Young of the Bureau of Economic Analysis for the questions which they answered in a timely, courteous and patient manner.

Overall constructive review and suggestions were furnished by Anirvan Banerji of the Center for International Business Cycle Research at Columbia University. Many if not most of his suggestions were adopted, which has resulted in a more complete presentation of relevant information.

Pamela van Giessen of Probus Publishing Company was appreciated greatly for her encouragement and patience in this undertaking.

PART I

INTRODUCTION TO INDICATORS

CHAPTER 1

INFORMATION, INDICATORS, AND BUSINESS CYCLES

Imagine the first man or woman on earth noticing what has become known as night and day. As the steady pattern of days and nights repeated, this first person became certain that day and night would occur. This certainty was a result of continued observations. The experience of the first days and weeks was probably one of terror and uncertainty. Certainty would not come until the over-and-over pattern repeated many times.

Since the beginning of time, people have desired to predict the future. Astrology, palm reading, tarot cards and the effect of sun spots and lunar cycles all have disciples, whose interest is future-oriented. Predictions of wars, political behavior, personal relationships, and business decisions are just a few areas addressed by the astute astrologer. The astrologer pays attention to the location of the planets, the palm reader to the length of the lifeline, and the tarot reader to the cards. All are observing what is taking place in the present with reference to the past. Based on what has happened in the past, a significant sign is looked for in the current observation, event or happening. This significant sign provides the basis for a forecast.

Opinions and/or decisions are flavored by experience based upon the store of observations. A larger number of observations increases the ability to arrive at a correct conclusion. Here the conclusion is intuitive, where intuition is defined as knowing without the use of rational processes.

On analyzing the thought processes by which intuitive decisions are made, the interpretation of information proceeds through several different stages before arriving at a decision. As more information is received, the probability of an event occuring can be categorized as follows:

- Remote
- Possible
- Probable
- Certain

Even though most of us do not formalize any estimate of a decision about whether an event is likely to occur, our past experience already provides this information to us. Whether one is aware of it or not, any decision one makes is based upon an assignment of an expected probability. If something is almost 95% certain to happen, our confidence level would assign a possibility of occurrence ranging from probable to certain.

Business decision makers desire forecasts based upon science rather than on intuition, or what many thought were areas of fantasy. The fields of statistics and econometrics provide method that use rational processes. Statistical methods can supply a more objective approach to this forecasting than the previous intuitive sort of probability assignment. These rational processes also involve the analysis of observations. In economics and accounting, observations are generally of a quantitative nature. Numbers provide the raw material from which conclusions may be inferred.

The purpose of forecasting is aptly described by Arthur B. Burns in *Frontiers of Economic Knowledge*, where he stated "the choice before man is not whether to engage in forecasting or to abstain, but whether to base expectations on hunches or on lessons distilled from experience."

OBSERVATIONS AND DATA PROCESSING

Meaningful information requires summarization. For example, each individual sales invoice of a department store would not be significant to a sales manager. Totals for the day, month, quarter, or year generally provide the needed information. The individual data observations are used to derive information that is more useful to users. The observations require processing to reach a point where analysis can commence. Data is summarized during data processing, with a large mass of data reduced to a number of observations that are hopefully more meaningful. It is for this reason that data has been called the raw material of information, while information is sometimes referred to as data made useful. This procedure and its results are shown below.

Exhibit 1-1

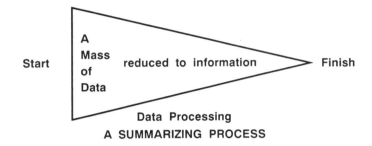

Start   A Mass of Data   reduced to information   Finish

Data Processing
A SUMMARIZING PROCESS

An example of this summarization involves the use of monthly data. To generate monthly data, one could total all the monthly data, and divide by the number of days, generating an average per day. In a thirty-day month, thirty days of data would be reduced to one average number, which one might accept as being representative of the thirty observations. One should realize that this summarization process has the effect of smoothing the results, since day-to-day fluctuations would not appear if averages were used.

If indicators are made from information that is a result of data processing, one should look for certain qualities to be present in both the data and the information.

INFORMATION QUALITY

The quality of information was addressed in the Financial Accounting Standards Board (1980) statement titled *Qualitative Characteristics of Accounting Information*, from which much of the following has been adapted. Since most of the data used in developing information is a result of accounting, these characteristics are important in any discussion of whether information disclosed is of value. Accounting information is normally processed for purposes of decision making. It makes no sense to process data for no other purpose than the process itself.

Data processing should supply information that:

- **costs less than the benefits** of having the information,
- **is material,** or makes a difference in the decision, and
- **is understandable** to an informed user.

Primary Qualities and Ingredients

The primary qualities that information should possess are those of **relevance and reliability**.

Relevance means that information must pertain to the decision making, and the particular information must be necessary in that it makes a difference. Its primary ingredients in terms of information are as follows:

- **Predictive value** - Should have some ability to help in making decisions, that are future oriented and not historical.
- **Feedback value** - Should provide a basis of comparison, such as comparing an actual with a forecasted value.
- **Timeliness** - Information must be available upon which to base decisions.

Reliability suggests different things to different people, but the framework sets forth the following characteristics:

- **Verifiability** - An ability to replicate information by using defined procedures.
- **Neutrality** - Freedom from bias.
- **Representational faithfulness** - Information represents that which it purports to represent, i.e., an item included in sales belongs in that total so that sales are not understated and that the stated total of sales is correct.

All of the above characteristics are important, but cost/benefit, materiality, and understandibility act as screening criteria for any selection of information on which to base decisions.

ACCOUNTS, TIME SERIES, MEASURES , AND INDICATORS

Most observations are the result of an accounting effort. In accounting, one puts all the information regarding one unique classification in what is called an **account**. This account is representative of that specific information. For purposes of updating, entries are made into this account at the end of certain regular intervals. The end result is a **time series.** A formal definition could be that a **time series represents a series of entries of information of the same classification or type, collected over time.** Updating increases the number of individual entries as well as changing the total account balance. All of these entries, as well as the account balance, measure what has happened to that unique classification over a defined time period. A simple definition of a measure could be as follows.

A measure is information, that provides knowledge of a particular, unique classification.

One should notice that the definition of a measure does not include any requirement of a definite size or amount of information. If the qualification of predictive value is added to this definition of a measure, one arrives at a simple definition of an indicator.

An indicator is a measure, that provides knowledge of a particular, unique classification of information that has predictive value.

INTERPRETATION OF INFORMATION

Time is a great determinant of the accuracy of any forecast. It is easy for most people to project their plans for the next day, week, or month, or even the next year. As the time becomes greater, so does the uncertainty because of the number of variables or factors that enter into any projection. A personal forecast would involve such considerations as occupation, health, marital status, and dependents. These factors can change with time. Assumptions can be made that will predict the future in one manner; but if one of these variables changes, the outcome becomes clouded and can differ dramatically. Because of the multidimensional aspects affecting decision making, the use of only one time series to provide predictive value is difficult.

TIME SERIES ANALYSIS

A time series must be analyzed to establish its value in terms of materiality and relevancy. This analysis involves dissecting a particular series to understand its various components. Dubois (1979) and Billingsley (1986) have identified these components as variations due to the following factors:

- Trend
- Cycle
- Seasonal
- Irregular

In illustrating the differences between these components, a time series of gross sales will be used. The particular time series for gross sales is from different companies in different industries, which best illustrates the particular time series component.

Trend

Trend refers to the long-term movement of a time series. Trends are affected by changes in population, inflation, business competition, and technology.

Exhibit 1-2

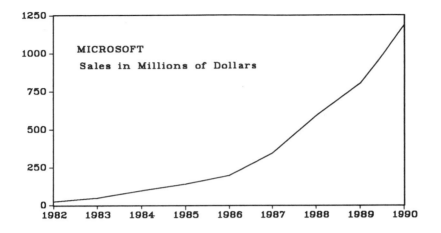

Notice that this time series exhibits a marked upward trend in sales, and is free of any noticeable cycle or recurring pattern. This is a pattern which many firms in new industries exhibit.

Cycle

Movements in a time series show a recurring pattern over a period greater than a year are referred to as cyclical variations.

Certain industries are cyclical in that their sales activities exhibit recurrent, marked expansion and contraction of sales. The following sales bar graph of Phelps Dodge, the largest producer of copper, shows how copper prices (line graph) have varied according to demand and the resultant effect on sales.

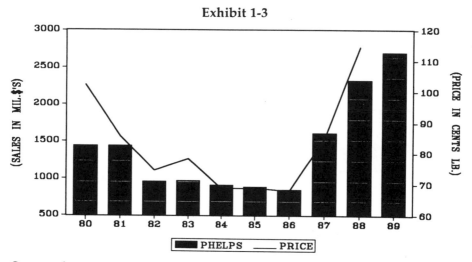

Exhibit 1-3

Seasonal

Seasonal variations can be identified by their recurrence at a particular time of year. Department store sales and sales of agricultural products are just a few industries that exhibit these characteristics.

This seasonality can be shown by the quarterly sales patterns of Mattel, Inc., one of the three largest domestic toy companies.

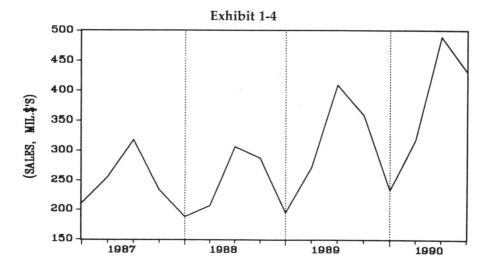

Exhibit 1-4

The extreme concentration of sales can easily be seen by the peak in activity at recurring times during the year.

It is important to realize that a particular time series may have all components present. The previous illustrations were used because the particular time series component was readily apparent. A company whose activities require much analysis to understand would be Bethlehem Steel, the nation's second largest steel producer. Forty years ago, this company's stock was rated A, but it has now fallen to a poor C rating.

Exhibit 1-5

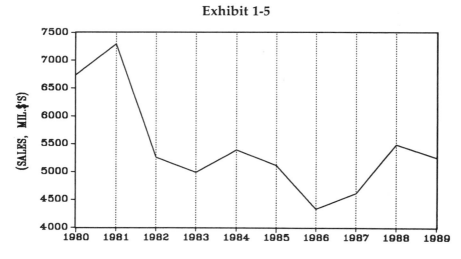

As indicated, there is an apparent decreasing trend, a cyclical effect, and organizational changes requiring extensive investigation.

Irregularities

Those movements that do not fit into any of the other categories are categorized as irregularities. Some of the most common causes are strikes, war, and government action.

DEVELOPING INDICATORS

Any organization can accumulate many time series during its course of existence. The time series could deal with sales, cost of sales, inventory, receipts, disbursements, or a variety of expenses such as gas and oil or administrative salaries. For most organizations, these time series represent totals (aggregates or sums). For instance, a large organization might have one total sales aggregate, but that total would be made up of many sales of different products or services.

Disaggregation

One must compare apples with apples, not apples with oranges. To explore and explain the relationship between different time series, a **disaggregation**, or breaking up of the sum into its respective components, should be undertaken. In the example of sales above, a prediction as to sales of Product A should be based on previous sales of Product A, not on the aggregate total of organization sales, which could include sales of other products.

This disaggregation is especially important in our complex organizational environment. Whether in the public or private sector, the organization of today has evolved into a manager's headache as it affects decision making. The number of variables to be considered in any decision has expanded rapidly. Very few organizations are focused, in the sense that only one product or service is rendered. Many focused organizations have done very well; and in the private sector, one finds that their operations are much more predictable as to earnings and finances.

The complexity of the modern organization can be observed by a look at the evolution of a business enterprise from its inception to its present state. Some of the factors which tend to explain some of the problems in forecasting are shown below.

FROM	TO
One Product	Many Products
One Industry	Multi-Industry
Few Competitors	Highly Competitive
Small Number of Employees	Large Numbers
Regional Operations	Multinational

It would seem that size, with its attendant complexity, should and does create more problems for the forecaster.

Methods of analyzing the relationship of variables to each other have been developed. Dubois (1979) and Billingsley (1986) both describe basic procedures using regression and correlation analysis.

The objective of regression analysis is to determine the functional relationship between variables. Correlation analysis measures the direction and strength of the relationship between the variables.

The works of Johnston (1984) and Pindyck (1990) describe more advanced methods for using statistical procedures for analyzing measures to establish predictive values.

The U.S. government has been interested in developing indicators for use in anticipating receipts and disbursements, as well as in allocating resources in such a way as to benefit the country. All government agencies collect and process tremendous amounts of data received as a result of mandated reports and returns. This information is furnished to interested parties at nominal cost. *The Bureau of Economic Analysis (BEA) of the Department of Commerce* is responsible for the collection and reporting of many of the indicators presented. The BEA has been especially active in work connected with research into business cycle activity, and in the analysis of indicators for the purpose of predicting possible peaks and troughs.

A business cycle has been defined as

> **recurrent sequences of cumulative expansions and contraction in various economic processes which are both sufficiently diffused and sufficiently synchronized to show up as major fluctuations in comprehensive measures of employment, production, income, and sales.**

(Zarnowitz and Boschan, 1977)

Table 1

Business Cycle Reference Dates		Duration in Months			
		Contraction		Cycle	
Trough	Peak	(Trough from Previous Peak)	Expansion (Trough to Peak)	Trough from Previous Trough	Peak from Previous Peak
December 1854	June 1854	....	30	....	....
December 1858	October 1860	18	22	48	40
June 1861	April 1865	8	*46*	30	*54*
December 1867	June 1869	*32*	18	*78*	50
December 1870	October 1873	18	34	36	52
March 1879	March 1882	65	36	99	101
May 1885	March 1887	38	22	74	60
April 1888	July 1890	13	27	35	40
May 1891	January 1893	10	20	37	30
June 1894	December 1895	17	18	37	35
June 1897	June 1899	18	24	36	42
December 1900	September 1902	18	21	42	39
August 1904	May 1907	23	33	44	56
June 1908	January 1910	13	19	46	32
January 1912	January 1913	24	12	43	36
December 1914	August 1918	23	*44*	35	*67*
March 1919	January 1920	*7*	10	51	17
July 1921	May 1923	18	22	28	40
July 1924	October 1926	14	27	36	41
November 1927	August 1929	13	21	40	34
March 1933	May 1937	43	50	64	*93*
June 1938	February 1945	13	*80*	63	93
October 1945	November 1948	*8*	37	88	45
October 1949	June 1953	11	45	48	56
May 1954	August 1957	*10*	39	55	49
April 1958	April 1960	8	24	47	32
February 1961	December 1969	10	*106*	34	*116*
November 1970	November 1973	*11*	36	*117*	47
March 1975	January 1980	16	58	52	74
July 1980	July 1981	6	12	64	18
November 1982	July 1990	16	92	28	108

Average, All Cycles:

1854-1982 (30 cycles)		18	[1]35	51	53
1854-1919 (16 cycles)		32	27	48	[2]49
1919-1945 (6 cycles)		18	35	53	53
1945-1982 (8 cycles)		11	[3]50	56	[3]61

Average, Peacetime Cycles:

1854-1982 (30 cycles)		19	[4]29	46	48
1854-1919 (16 cycles)		22	24	46	[5]47
1919-1945 (6 cycles)		20	26	46	45
1945-1982 (8 cycles)		11	[6]43	46	[6]63

1.	31 cycles	3.	9 cycles	5.	13 cycles
2.	15 cycles	4.	26 cycles	6.	7 cycles

Note: Figures printed in bold italic are the wartime expansions (Civil War, World Wars I and II, Korean War and Vietnam War), the postwar contractions, and the full cycles that include the wartime expansions.

(National Bureau of Economic Research, Inc.)

BUSINESS CYCLES IN THE UNITED STATES

The study of business cycles has been greatly influenced by the work of Wesley C. Mitchell in his 1913 book titled *Business Cycles* and by Arthur F. Burns and Wesley C. Mitchell in their major collaboration , *Measuring Business Cycles.*

In 1920, Wesley C. Mitchell and others helped to organize the National Bureau of Economic Reseach (NBER). This independent, nonprofit organization maintains an active and continuing interest in business cycle analysis. NBER, through its seven member Business Cycle Dating Committee, is responsible for dating of the business cycle peaks and troughs. The results of this committee's actions are the most authoritative in the United States. Academics and others have argued about other dates being the most precise, but differences do not seem to be that large. Announcements of peak and trough dates are many months after the selected date. This lag is caused by the need to validate the actions of some indicators by the actions of others. A tabulation of peak and trough dates compiled by NBER is shown in Table 1-1. Some questions may be answered by reference to this exhibit. How long is the usual contraction and the expansion phase, and how long does it take from one peak to another peak, on average?

The preceding study and the following graph should serve to answer some of the questions posed previously.

Exhibit 1-6

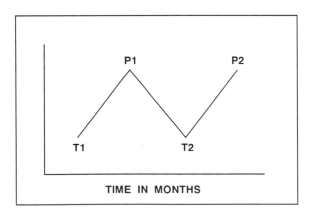

By reference to the study, one finds that the average length in peace-time from T1 to P1 for all cycles (expansion phase) would be 29 months. Further, the average length of the contraction phase from P1 to T2 is 19 months. The overall length from peak to peak would be 48 (29+19) months.

This information gives an average, but averages can be misleading. If government action intervenes, a normal economic contraction and ex-pansion phase can be postponed. This prolonged expansion phase is noted for all the war years. If indicators signalled a faltering economy and there was confidence in the signals being generated by the indica-tors, government intervention could result in postponement of that ex-pected downturn in activity through action. A few examples of government intervention are as follows:

- Lengthening unemployment insurance benefits, which has the effect of maintaining consumer expenditures

- Extending spending programs, that have been scheduled for elimination to preserve jobs, such as military cutbacks

- Giving immediate tax breaks for spending in areas desired to be encouraged, such as investment tax credits or shorter ap-proved service lives for depreciable assets

- Decreasing interest rates to encourage consumption and invest-ment

Since November, 1982, the U.S. had been in an expansion phase. This phase through July 1990 was of 92 months duration. Looking at the aver-ages, one sees that this latest expansion phase was far greater than the usual 29 months. This cycle is greater than any other expansion cycle except during the Vietnam War. The contraction phase from July 1981 to November 1982 was of 16 months' duration. This is not far off the aver-age for modern periods. The expansion phase came at a time when there was no war. Several clues exist as to why this prosperity phase contin-ued, but the best explanation seems to be the large increase in the federal deficit from 1983 onward, as shown below.

Year	Federal Deficit (In Billions $'s)
1983	230.8
1984	218.2
1985	266.4
1986	283.0
1987	222.4
1988	252.9

Source: U.S. Department of Treasury

The largest previous budget deficit was in 1982, when the deficit was only $134.2 billion. Clearly, government intervention was on a grand scale. The prolonged prosperity was purchased in a similar manner as when an individual lives it up by getting loans.

CAUSES OF PEAKS IN BUSINESS CYCLES

Many economists have investigated the causes of peaking in a business cycle. Eckstein and Sinai (1986) categorized events that precede recessions as arising out of the following events:

- Boom periods, when demand has risen above the long-term trend, causing capacity constraints;

- Demand shocks, which are caused by a sudden lessening demand;

- Supply shocks, which are caused by curtailment of supplies or other disruptions. (The steel strike in 1959, the auto strike in 1970, and the disruption in world oil supplies in 1973 and 1978 are illustrative of these shocks.);

- Price shocks, which are created by movements outside normal supply and demand relationships. (Price controls can be responsible for this sort of event.); and

- Credit crunches, where financial distress is reflected in lessened availability of money and credit.

LEADING, COINCIDENT, AND LAGGING INDICATORS

The Bureau of Economic Analysis has many time series that are analyzed for relevancy. It has grouped these time series into series that exhibit the characteristics of leading, coincident, or lagging indicators.

To analyze the business economy the Bureau used many different time series. As the Bureau analyzed the different time series, the time series were classified as to their usefulness in predicting business cycles peaks and troughs. The classifications provided time series categorized by:

- **Leading Indicators** that were most capable of predicting peaks or troughs in advance,

- **Co-incident** indicators for time series, whose changing values take place at the time of a peak of trough, and

- **Lagging** indicators, whose action lags that of the leading and coincident indicators.

In studying the indicators, one should develop a feeling about the predicative values of a particular time series in particular situations. Necessarily, one should try to come up with the best indicator for use in a particular situation. A look at the indicators used by the Bureau of Economic Analysis will show how these indicators are used and that possibly not all indicators must be used. If one can eliminate any variables, one can simplify the forecasting procedures necessary to provide answers. This elimination can result in a more effective method rather than just elimination for the purpose of simplification.

Moore and Shiskin (1967) developed and applied the indicator system. This system was re-appraised by Zarnowitz and Boschan (1977). The following definitions and descriptions of leading, coincident, and lagging indicators are from that collaboration.

Leading Indicators

Leading indicators represent anticipation and early links in the sequences of business decisions, early stages of the investment and production processes, and measures of flows contribution to changes in the levels of economic stocks. This tendency to lead makes them obvious warning signals and tools for the forecasting of changes in general business conditions. Their main shortcomings are their hypersensitivity and the considerable variation in the length of their leads, particularly before business cycle peaks. Also to the extent that warning signs are heeded by policy makers, the forecasting effectiveness becomes impaired as counter-cyclical measures are implemented.

Coincident Indicators

Coincident indicators are broad comprehensive measures which tend to summarize the state of actual business activity from the input and output side. They not only confirm or invalidate expectations based on the behavior of the leading indicators but also give some precision to the timing of the broad swings in economic activity. It is the behavior of the coincident that should firm up policy decision that the leaders could only suggest.

Lagging Indicators

The first function of the lagging indicators is to confirm or refute the inferences derived from the behavior of the coincident indicators. Perhaps more important for forecasting purposes, however, is the characteristic lead of the laggers relative to the opposite turns of the leaders. Many lagging indicators, such as interest rates charged by banks, unit labor costs, inventories carried in manufacturing and trade, and business loans outstanding, measure or reflect the cost of doing business. It is mainly for this reason that these series, when inverted, lead most of the other important indicators (not only the coincident but often also the leaders). For example, declines in inventories and interest rates during a business contraction pave the way for an upturn in new orders and then in the output of materials, etc., by making business operations less expensive and hence potentially more profitable, and also by depleting stock relative to the current production and sales requirement.

Economic Processes

The definition of business cycles includes a requirement that expansions and contractions be diffused throughout the economy. Indicators are categorized by the particular economic process to which they apply, so that the extent of diffusion may be studied. These processes and subcategories are described in later chapters. Fabozzi and Greenfield (1984) provide detailed descriptions of the economic processes and the effect of indicators representing subcategories within that process.

A SCORING SYSTEM

The present system of appraising indicators was first developed and applied by Moore and Shiskin (1967). The work of Zarnowitz and Boschan (1977) described the principles upon which the present scoring system is based. This scoring uses six criteria in assessing and selecting indicators. These criteria are as follows:

Economic Significance - How well understood and how important is the role in the business cycle of the variable represented by the data?

Statistical Adequacy - How well does the given series measure the economic variable or process in question?

Timing at Revivals and Recessions - How consistently has the series led, coincided, or lagged at the successive business cycle turns?

Conformity to Historical Business Cycles - How regularly have the movements in the specific indicators reflected the expansion and contraction in the economy at large?

Smoothness - How well is cyclical direction shown without being obscured by large erratic variations?

Currency or Timeliness - How promptly available are the statistics and how frequently are they reported?

The scores of various indicators are shown at the end of the various chapters, after classification by economic process, and with a description of the particular indicator.

Many of the criteria used for scoring are also used by accountants to judge the quality of information. One could match economic significance with materiality, statistical adequacy with representational faithfulness, timing with consistency, and conformity and timeliness to timeliness. This emphasis on the quality of information with which to work cannot be overemphasized.

DATA AND INFORMATION PROBLEMS

Actions of indicators affect decision making. Any indicator's value is determined by the accuracy of data used in the development of the indicator. Reliability and relevancy are the quality standards by which data and resulting indicator value should be judged. Evaluation of data collection and statistical methods used to develop data and/or indicators can provide some estimate as to reliability.

An example of a statistic, that is eagerly awaited, that affects decision making, and that has serious reliability questions is the Gross National Product (GNP). This indicator is of a quarterly nature and is subject to many revisions, and preliminary estimates regularly differ from the final revised figures. In November 1991, major revisions were made to the National Income and Product Accounts (NIPA).

Problems in the collection of data were reported by the Bureau of Labor Statistics (BLS) in November 1991. The BLS found that it had counted 650,000 jobs that did not seem to exist. Indicators based on employment figures that included these nonexistent jobs would be very inaccurate.

Many of the indicators represent totals of other indicators, and a misstatement of one of the underlying indicators can make the total almost meaningless. At times, one is perplexed by seeming discrepancies between amounts reported in previous years as compared with present tables that contain historical information. The best way to overcome this frustration is to verify the data source, and then to use the new data, which is more reliable since it is based on the latest available information.

INDICATORS FOR A CHANGING ENVIRONMENT

Change is a part of everyone's life. As one lives through change, differences seem gradual. These differences can cause information to lose its past importance and relevancy. The rate at which change is taking place gives some indication of the need to be always watchful of the reliability of information and of the associated indicators providing information that has predictive value. Geoffrey Moore in *Leading Indicators for the 1990s* (1990) addresses the effects of a changing environment on indicators. To illustrate the rapidity of change, one only has to look at the past.

Alvin Toffler in *Future Shock* (1970) supplied information from which the following has been adapted.

RATE AND MAGNITUDE OF CHANGE

MAN'S EXISTENCE HAS BEEN ESTIMATED AT **50,000** YEARS. A LIFETIME IS APPROXIMATELY 62 YEARS.

800 LIFETIMES

OF THESE 800 LIFETIMES

- **650** WERE SPENT IN CAVES.

- ONLY IN THE LAST **70** HAVE WE HAD WRITTEN COMMUNICATION.

- ONLY IN THE LAST **6** HAVE WE HAD MASS PRINTING CAPABILITY.

- ONLY IN THE LAST **4** HAVE WE BEEN ABLE TO MEASURE TIME ACCURATELY.

- ONLY IN THE LAST **2** HAVE WE HAD ELECTRIC MOTORS.

- **MOST MATERIAL GOODS WE USE IN DAILY LIFE HAVE BEEN DEVELOPED IN THIS, THE 800TH LIFETIME.**

Toffler also believes that with better communication methods, the time needed to transfer ideas or theories to the factory floor and new product innovation is shortened dramatically. The rate of change is accelerating, making environmental change even more dynamic than in the past. Robert Solow won the Nobel Prize for his work, which stressed that leading technology is more important than the amount of capital in driving a nation's economic growth. In *Powershift* (1990), Toffler describes some of his visions of the future. This future differs in many respects from the present, and the differences further underscore the need to examine data relevancy as to the future and not to the past, except for its historical value.

THE YEARS AHEAD

New products and methods of accomplishing tasks will continue to be developed at an ever increasing rate. These changes must be analyzed for their effect on indicators and information to assure their relevancy to the present. Additional measures must be tested to find out if more indicators are available. These sources must be reliable, and their findings available in a timely manner.

ENVIRONMENTAL, ECOLOGICAL, AND POLITICAL CHANGES

The activities and influence of groups concerned with clean air, the preservation of natural habitats, and the disappearance of animal and plant life can be expected to increase in the years ahead. Conflict between what is desirable in the way of quality of life and what is affordable is sure to take place. Reality will temper the accomplishments desired by the utopian visionaries, but changes are certain. Changes in the whats, wheres, hows, and whys of product development and manufacture will almost certainly replace many of our present industries with new and yet unknown activities. Politically, the federal deficit, an aging population, education, and crime are just a few issues that may require new solutions, and new indicators may be needed to monitor these new happenings.

Major changes in cyclical behavior and their effects are discussed in detail by Zarnowitz and Moore (1986). This work provides valuable insights into how cyclical behavior has been altered by structural, institutional, and political changes.

A CHANGING WORLD ENVIRONMENT

Aside from the consideration of new products and services, the 1990s promise to offer many changes in the world environment. One should realize that because of the increases in the speed at which communication takes place, oceans do not create barriers to change.

The changes seen as affecting our future lives are based upon the way in which investors, workers, entrepreneurs, organizations, and politicians adjust to meet individual and national self-interest. Material issues of importance are:

- The unification of Germany

- The European Common Market

- Emerging Third World Nations

- The changing political makeup of many nations from a controlled-market (communistic) to a free-market (capitalistic) economy

- A possible change in the use of resources within a nation because of increased perceptions of peaceful co-existence. This could result in lower military budgets, and the possible use of these funds to address societal problems, or to reduce the budget deficit.

All of these issues will make changes in the where, why, and how capital, people, and resources are employed. Previous theories or preferences may have to be revised about the interpretation of data, especially its materiality and interpretation. Indicators such as interest rates, foreign-exchange rates, exports and imports, and spending patterns within a nation are just a few of the areas which could be subject to a great deal of variation in the years ahead.

INTEREST AND FOREIGN-EXCHANGE RATES

As the size of any country's economy increases (relative to the world economies), the influence of that particular nation or group of nations' activities should increase greatly.

With the unification of Germany and the European Common Market, two large economies will be present. These larger-than-previous economies will create their own demand and supply needs for money and credit. Because of their perceived size and political stabilility, they could quite possibly attract investors previously looking only to the U.S. as the largest and safest haven for investment funds. This could result in a decline in the importance of the dollar and a possible increase in interest rates in the U.S. to compete. The key lies in how international investors view these nations in terms of size and stability.

The possible adoption of a common currency by members of the European Common Market could also introduce increased financing in that newly created monetary unit. Competition could increase interest rates, especially when one considers the demands for capital from changing economies and third world nations.

EXPORTS AND IMPORTS

The European Common Market objectives are the elimination of national boundaries in trade, and the possible introduction of a common currency. The effects of change on export and import patterns are difficult to ascertain since many U.S. multinational corporations are a part of this structure through ownership of foreign subsidiaries. Possibly, the greatest influence could be in the area of interest rates, where a common currency could also allow for financing in that currency unit.

CHANGING SPENDING PATTERNS

Hopefully, if the need for governments to spend money for one purpose is not present, the money can be used for other necessary purposes. This could be done without increasing taxes and represents a redeployment of resources. An example of this would be a change in the perceived need for the large military budget in the U.S. If some money were diverted to the budget deficit and a lowering of debt, the U.S. might not be the only safe haven for investment funds, but at least it would be one of the best.

CHAPTER 2

ADJUSTMENTS TO TIME SERIES DATA

The purpose of data processing is to provide information useful in decision making. This processing is usually undertaken by a party who is not the decision maker. The preparer might be an accountant, an economist, or a statistician. Since data processing renders a service, the objective should be to provide the best information possible. Information must be communicated to be understood. To meet that objective, indicators can be presented in different ways or derived by adjusting time series data. These derived indicators can be more easily understood and can supply more relevant information than the original time series from which they were constructed. Some methods of presentation and types of derived indicator are as follows:

- Seasonally adjusted
- Change
- Rate of Change
- Moving Averages
- Exponentially Smoothed
- Index Numbers
- Diffusion Indexes

To aid in decision making, it may be desirable to include many different methods and derivations of the same series. A study of this type can facilitate the work of the user by providing confirmation or validation to a previous hypothesis.

METHOD OF PRESENTATION

Instead of modifying the data, one can elect to present the same graph using an arithmetic or a logarithmic scale. These two presentation methods follow.

Exhibit 2-1

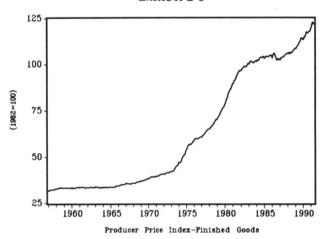

Producer Price Index—Finished Goods

The above graph is an example of an arithmetic scale, where the intervals between values 25, 50, and 75 are the same. The next scale shown is logarithmic, with intervals between values changing according to the percentage change in value. The range from 25 to 50 on the above scale represents a 100% change; but from 50 to 75, the change in percent is only 50%. The intervals on the logarithmic scale make the interval between 50 and 75 only one-half the size of the interval between 25 and 50.

Logarithmic scales are a valuable aid in assessing materiality of change. Notice in year 1990+, the arithmetic scale shows a much steeper slope than the logarithmic scale. To the eye, the arithmetic scale can mislead a user as to the extent that change is material.

Exhibit 2-2

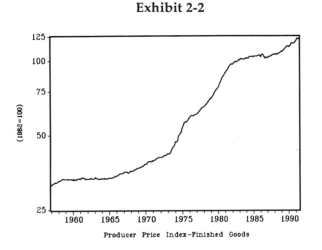

Producer Price Index-Finished Goods

SEASONALITY

Raw data exhibits certain characteristics, including seasonality. By eliminating seasonal effects, the individual observation may be more easily compared and examined, for trends and cyclical and irregular components.

The following graph shows the Producers' Price Index, seasonally and non-seasonally adjusted.

Exhibit 2-3

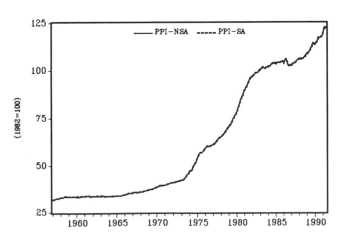

As shown above, sometimes the differences between seasonally adjusted and nonseasonally adjusted numbers are not apparent. In this case, it is because of the long time period involved and the large range in values.

To show the differences more effectively, one could limit the time period, and some of the differences will show up more readily.

Exhibit 2-4

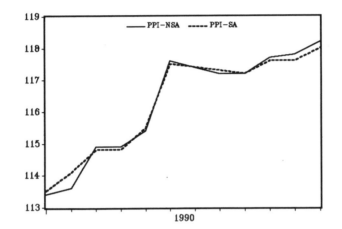

CHANGE

The difference in the dollar amounts between a particular period is easy to envision. Subtraction of one amount from another amount will result in the change for the period under review. The dollar amounts used are a result of averaging, so as to smooth out some of the irregularities that may occur in changes for only a few days. One widely reported change indicator is shown next.

Exhibit 2-5

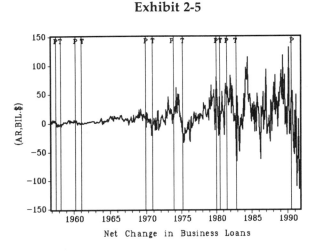

Net Change in Business Loans

Notice that materiality is easier to identify using a change indicator than an indicator showing only total loans. It may be that, over time, a specific amount of change has been identified as being critical. If this were true, a change indicator would be very helpful in deciding what areas of the economy are particulary affected. In cases such as this, materiality would be more evident; and the use of a rate of change indicator would make an indicator more understandable.

RATE OF CHANGE

A modification of the previous change time series would result in a time series expressed as a percentage. A simple adjustment will supply the percentage increase or decrease from one period to another. The BEA has rate of changes for most major indicators (See Appendix 1).

One of these change indicators is shown next.

Exhibit 2-6

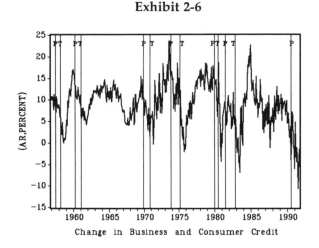

Change in Business and Consumer Credit

The objective is to make the change apparent in an easy to understand manner. Materiality can be explored easily, and the possible significance of a percentage change at various peaks and troughs is more easily discovered.

MOVING AVERAGES

Most of the indicators used are of a monthly nature because of the requirement of timeliness. The monthly information is a result of what took place during that month. This monthly information is close to what is taking place currently, or at least closer than what transpired during a longer term. In many cases, it is desirable to look at both short- and long-term trends. To accomplish this, a month span and a six-month span might be constructed.

The moving averages contrasted below illustrate the results achieved using this procedure.

Exhibit 2-7

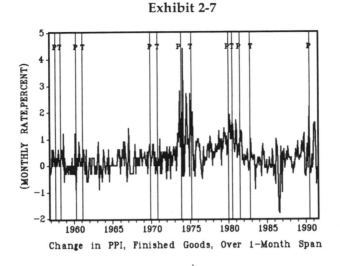

Change in PPI, Finished Goods, Over 1-Month Span

Contrast the above with the longer span below.

Exhibit 2-8

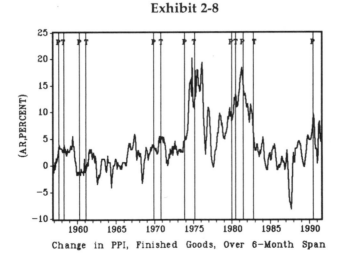

Change in PPI, Finished Goods, Over 6-Month Span

The smoothing out of the irregular patterns is evident in the six-month span. One should be careful in using the smoother spans by themselves, as present important trends may be obscured.

EXPONENTIAL SMOOTHING

Moving averages result in equal credit given to old as well as new observations. Exponential smoothing allows the processor to assign various weights in the computation to the latest observations. This would result in an indicator that could be closer to current values, depending upon the weight assigned to the current value. This process is utilized in the indicator as shown below.

Exhibit 2-9

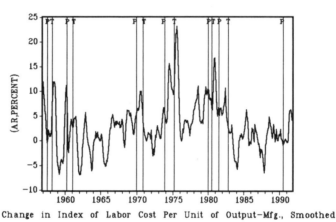

Change in Index of Labor Cost Per Unit of Output—Mfg., Smoothed

INDEX NUMBERS

Index numbers are widely used to reduce other time series to a more useful indicator. Index numbers express a relationship between two numbers, with one number referred to as a base number. The most familiar index number is the Consumer Price Index (CPI).

An index number may be either simple or composite. A simple index number uses only one time series in its construction, while a composite combines a number of related time series into a new single time series and establishes a reference to a specific base year. The Consumer Price Index and Producers' Price Index are both examples of composite index numbers, since they are constructed of many different prices of many different goods. Indexes can be further classified by their type. These types are as follows:

- Price index numbers, which deal with changes in price only
- Quantity index numbers, which measure change in volume, such as the Index of Industrial Production
- Value index numbers, which reflect changes in both quantity and value. Gross National Product is an example of this type of index number.

Price index numbers are of general use in reducing or deflating an original indicator in current dollars to a base year. The BEA uses 1982 as a base year for the construction of constant dollar indexes. With the change in the National Income and Product Accounts base year to 1987, there is a probability of change in this base year for greater conformity.

DIFFUSION INDEXES

A change in one indicator doesn't necessarily mean that a change is present throughout the whole economy. A diffusion index may be constructed, that will show how widespread or diffused change is throughout the whole economy. Moore (1979) defines the construction of this type of index expressed as a percentage. The diffusion index is a composite index number with its components consisting of relevant time series. If most of the composite indicators are rising, the percentage derived will be greater than 50% or vice-versa. The spans can be adjusted to show short- and long-term movements and are illustrated using the following diffusion indexes:

Exhibit 2-10

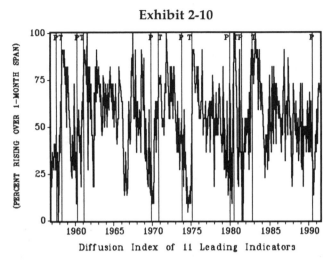

Diffusion Index of 11 Leading Indicators

A longer span may be desired.

Exhibit 2-11

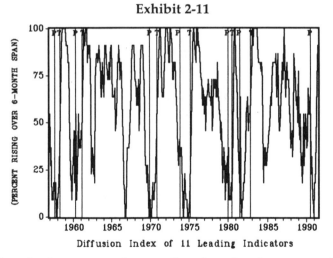

Diffusion Index of 11 Leading Indicators

Notice that the longer span is smoother than the shorter span because of the longer-term averaging.

OTHER DERIVED INDICATORS

Instead of one indicator, many indicators may be grouped together; and a composite index constructed. This type of indicator is discussed in a later chapter.

CHAPTER 3

SOURCES OF INFORMATION

To use data in decision making, it must be gathered, processed, and reported in a useful manner. Hopefully, the results will contain many of the qualities that have been discussed previously, especially relevancy, reliability, and materiality. One has seen a tremendous increase in the number of vendors of information. This increase of available information has been a result of the invention of the microprocessor, which made the microcomputer possible. Microcomputers make the processing, recording, and manipulation of data easier for parties that previously did not have access to large computer systems. The new computers are also at work in areas such as publishing, affecting the speed at which the printed word can be communicated. The acceleration of communications results in knowledge becoming available for use earlier and allows one to base decision making upon information that is more current, which is generally more reliable.

PRINTED DATA

Many different sources for printed data are available. Updating a time series is very important because using the latest information available will provide the best solutions. Using printed data for updating time series requires discipline, and close attention to data entry, and it could be frustrating if some data items are missing. With a few time series, it would be easy to stay on top of these difficulties. If an analysis covers twenty or more indicators, use of a database service is recommended. The following are just a few of the sources for printed material.

Newspapers

For the person interested only in a few data items of national significance like stock, commodity, or financial information, an easy source would be a national newspaper that has an extensive financial reporting section. Some of these newspapers, either daily or weekly, are:

Wall Street Journal
Barron's
New York Times
Media General

For regional data, local newspapers and trade publications can supply the most current information available.

Regularly Published Sources

Some services specialize in the publication of information on a continuing basis. Each issue does not normally delete previous data but just updates the data, resulting in continuity in any data series and eliminating the frustration of possible missed data. Their services are specialized, but one finds excellent data sources available from:

Standard and Poor's
Moody's
Value Line
Commodity Research Bureau
McGraw-Hill Information Services
Center for International Business Cycle Research

Standard and Poor's Corporation also publishes a *Statistical Service*, which includes time series and other financial information of a historical nature.

Governmental and Quasi-Governmental Publications

Some of the most reasonable and reliable sources of regular information are governmental and quasi-governmental publications. Some of the publications used by the author and recommended highly are:

The Survey of Current Business, a monthly publication, is published by the United States Department of Commerce and the Bureau of Economic Analysis. This survey contains information, graphs, charts, and tables about cyclical indicators as well as detailed data which disaggregates (breaks apart) many of the gross numbers into individual components.

Economic Indicators is published monthly for the joint Economic Committee by the Council of Economic Advisors. This is a smaller publication than the *Survey of Current Business*, but it summarizes much of the information; and it also includes information not included in the survey, but available through other sources that are deemed relevant.

Federal Reserve Publication is a monthly publication with historical data. It is important to anyone requiring money, credit, or other financial market information.

International data are available from a variety of sources. The International Monetary Fund (IMF), The Organization for Economic Co-operation and Development (OECD), and the United Nations (UN) all have publications written in many languages and are available at reasonable cost.

All of the government publications are available by subscription through the U.S. Government Printing Office. Since the quality of these publications and their price is reasonable, most libraries of any size carry current issues and have past issues available in bound form or on microfiche.

An important annual reference publication available at nominal cost is the *Statistical Abstract of the United States*, published by the *U.S. Department of Commerce, Bureau of the Census*. This publication is especially valuable because the tables supply names of sources, which can be used to supply additional needed details for review.

Trade Journals

Many trade and industry publications supply information that is invaluable in developing or using indicators representative of specialized segments of the economy. The *Oil and Gas Journal* specializes in the petroleum industry, and very complete information is available through this source.

ELECTRONIC TRANSMISSION

As the ability to process data became available because of the microcomputer, the demand for information to be accessed via phone lines and satellite increased. This has resulted in the formation and expansion of firms whose function is to supply data to users through communication devices from their processing plants thousands of miles away from a user's computer. The data supplied comes from the firm's database, which is nothing more than an inventory of data properly categorized for easy access. This information can be accessed through the use of a **modem.** This device converts data stored on another computer to data capable of being transmitted and understood by the receiver's computer.

Costs

Cost varies with the type of data accessed. A very specialized database would have a larger charge for its usage. Generally, total access cost is a function of the following:

- Distance Charged
- Basic Charge
- Connect Time
- Time of Day

Distance is not usually a large factor in the total data retrieval cost. A database may be located on the East Coast, but usually a large database provides a local phone number, so that the effect of distance is not material.

The two largest costs are usually the connect time and the basic charge. It is important to realize that even though a rate could be $100 per hour, the computer at the database organization can sort and sift in seconds and thus connect time could be very short. As a user acquires greater ability in using a particular database, the data desired can be accessed even faster.

The time of the day affects the bill. Most databases are available evenings and weekends at much lower rates than in the daytime. Avoiding peak charges is one way to reduce a database transmission bill dramatically.

The Benefits

Data can be accessed from a database and written to a disk on the user's computer. That disk file can then be exported into most popular computer programs available to a user. The result can be a constantly updated file, without manual entry, available within seconds. The database company verifies data, thus eliminating the possibility of transcribing errors, which could be present if inputted manually by the user from newspapers, services, or other publications.

SOME DATABASE ORGANIZATIONS

Different firms specialize in different databases. Some of the firms have a large inventory of databases, which cover a variety of subjects. One of the largest, one-stop databases is *Dialog Information Service*, which has databases not only in financial areas by also in science, engineering, medicine, and the social sciences. Its directory lists the databases, usage cost, and the type of information available. A small yearly charge, with most of the charges for connect time, is applied to different databases. This one-stop access is shown by the following databases available through Dialog, namely:

>Cendata
>Econbase: Time Series and Forecasts
>PTS International Forecasts
>PTS U.S. Forecasts
>PTS U.S. Time Series
>Media General Plus
>Disclosure
>Moody's Corporate Profiles

More databases are providing increased choices for their users. The narrow databases offered previously by various firms are giving way to the many databases with one-stop access as per the Dialog operation.

For specialized databases, one has more choices. For users it depends upon whether current or historical data is needed and how far back the data is available. Databases included in this category would be the following:

Dow Jones Retrieval is a service of Dow Jones, which publishes the *Wall Street Journal*. It contains current and historical information and also important news relative to subject matter of importance.

Dial Data is asource of historical and current data on securities and commodities.

Warner Communications has historical and current data on securities and commodities.

Citibase has a database of over 5600 economic time series. This represents one of the largest easily available economic databases in the United States.

Bureau of Economic Analysis has an electronic bulletin board, which can be accessed for most of the time series.

Compustat contains financial information from SEC filings and the annual and quarterly reports of most important publicly owned corporations in the U.S. This is a division of Standard and Poor's Corporation.

CRSP is a database maintained by the Center for Research in Security Prices. This database is invaluable in any study of returns over time for securities in the U.S.

Commodity Research Bureau has data covering both cash and futures commodity prices.

Haver Analytics provides access to thousands of time series. Specialized databases are offered, such as those developed by The Conference Board, National Association of Realtors, and the Center for International Business Cycle Research.

The above list includes only a few of the databases available. Many other government and private sector databases have some arrangements for computer access through bulletin boards. Many of the commercially available databases merely access the government material and offer the same for sale through their service. Others have developed proprietary series, which have proven to be helpful.

Data Use

With access to a database, it is an easy process to transfer this data from the remote database to a disk file on a microcomputer. Because of the tremendous increase in the number of users, the database organizations have adopted methods of writing the data to the disk on the microcomputer in a format acceptable by many major software packages. Lotus 123, Microsoft Excel, and other graphics and statistical packages are supported by these data vendors. These vendors also allow for a choice of other formats, which can be easily adapted by user programs for other software programs.

COMPUTER DISKS AND TAPES

More and more organizations are supplying information on diskette or tape, which allows the user easy access to historical data that is updated on receipt of the new diskette. With the expanded use of the compact disk, many large database companies are selling data in this form as an alternative to transmitted data. The Bureau of Economic Analysis has a diskette service that costs approximately $45. These disks supply many years of data and most series supported by BEA. Its content is shown in Appendix 1, and it is recommend as a very good source for indicator information of a national character. It is probable that connect time to reproduce the information on disk would cost a great deal more. The future is sure to see large amounts of data available on compact disks. As prices decrease for compact disk hardware, this media for micros will probably be one of the most often used sources of historical information. Most database organizations mentioned previously can supply disks, tapes, or hard copy to meet specific needs.

DATA CONVERSION

Data can become available through diskette or by downloading from a remote location via a modem. Once the data arrives, it may require further processing to be usable in a specific format. Many of the conversion programs in the academic area are written in Fortran, a programming language. For more efficient conversion, the C language is used quite extensively. The problem with both Fortran and C is that they both require an investment of both time and money. The one language that comes with almost every IBM PC or clone is BASIC. The Microsoft version is called GWBASIC, while the IBM version is BASICA. The manuals that come with almost all computers, as well as simple, available how-to books, provide instructions in creating simple programs for conversion of data. For this reason, the following applications program is written in GWBASIC, which is compatible with all MS-DOS microcomputers.

The Applications Program

The program converts the BEA disks into a format understood by most programs, namely an ASCII file, with values separated by commas. All major software packages supply the structure of the files, which they are capable of reading. This program could be adapted to many different user needs.

The program includes more remarks than code. This is to explain the structure of the code and also to provide some answers to how the code might be changed, to allow for different data file formats. In addition, this program contains procedures which may be repeated. Rather than explain more advanced programming techniques, this repetition is used to show how one can use a routine repeatedly and simply. It results in a program that is effective, but it may not be as efficient if optimized by advanced procedures.

Many commands used do not require certain words; but to make them more understandable, these words are included. A specific example is the use of the LET statement. One can say X=2, and this is permissible; however for understandability, LET X=2 is adopted. These are unnecessary remarks and commands and can be eliminated if desired.

Data File Layouts

An organization furnishing data will provide a description of their data file structure. This file structure is necessary to properly prepare a program to convert data to a format understood by the software used. The data file layout furnished by the BEA for their Business Cycle Indicators (BCI) file is as follows:

BCI Data File Layout

Record 1 — Title record

POSITION	FIELD
1-6	Series identification code
7	Not used
8-119	Alphanumeric series title
120	Not used

Record 2 — Descriptor Record

POSITION	FIELD
1-6	Series identification code
1-10	Not used
11-16	Date of most recent series update or revision
17-20	Not used
21-22	Beginning month of series (01-12)
23-24	Beginning year of series
25-26	Last data month of series (01-12)
27-28	Last data year of series
29-30	Reporting period code: 1 - Monthly 2 - Bi-monthly 3 - Quarterly 6 - Semi-annually 12 - Annually
31	Not used
32	Number of Decimal places in data (0-6) (needed with FORTRAN print formats)
33-120	Not used

Record 3 — Data Record

POSITION	FIELD
1-6	Series identification code
7	Not used
	DATA FIELDS
8-17	January data value
18-27	February data value
28-37	March data value
38-47	April data value
48-57	May data value
58-67	June data value
68-77	July data value
78-87	August data value
88-97	September data value
98-107	October data value
108-117	November data value
118-127	December data value

Looking at the data file layout, one notices that there are three records for each file. Files one and two contain descriptive information, while file three contains the data. The files are furnished in four different files on two diskettes, which can be easily copied to a hard disk.

By reading positions 1-6 in file one, one would access the series identification number. Note that this is the same on all three records. The purpose of knowing the position of the data on the particular record is so that one can access the correct information. March data are in record 3, positions 28-37. The method of accessing in BASIC is by use of commands such as LEFT$ and MID$. In line 1410 of the code, the series title is defined as MID$(RECORD$,8,112). By reference to the data file layout, the portion of the alphanumeric series title is 8-119, which represents 112 characters (119-8)+1=112. The VAL command converts string values to a numeric value, and can be used with a LEFT$ or MID$ command as shown in line 1520.

For any commands not easily understood, the BASIC manual supplied with your microcomputer should provide easy answers to any data conversion program.

```
1000 REM *********************************************** ****************
1010 REM    PROGRAM TO ACCESS BCD DISKS
1020 REM *********************************************** ****************
1030 COLOR 14,1,1 'TURNS ON COLOR IF MONITOR PRESENT
1040 DIM A#(12)
1050 KEY OFF:CLS 'TURNS OFF KEYS AT BOTTOM AND CLEARS SCREEN
1060 REM   SETS UP A MENU FOR EASIER USE
1070 REM *********************************************** ****************
1080 CLS:LOCATE 10,20:PRINT "CONVERSION AND PRINT PROGRAM"
1090 LOCATE 11,20:PRINT "————————————————————————"
1100 LOCATE 12,20:PRINT "CHOOSE ONE OF THE FOLLOWING"
1110 LOCATE 13,20:PRINT " 1. SERIES TO CONVERT"
1120 LOCATE 14,20:PRINT " 2. PRINTOUT OF SERIES"
1130 LOCATE 15,20:PRINT " 3. RETURN TO SYSTEM PROMPT"
1140 LOCATE 16,20:PRINT "————————————————————————"
1150 LOCATE 17,20:INPUT;CHOICE$ 'ACCEPTS USER INPUT
1160 IF CHOICE$="1" THEN CLS:GOTO 1210 'DATA VALIDATION
1170 IF CHOICE$="2" THEN CLS: GOTO 1920
1180 IF CHOICE$="3" THEN CLS: SYSTEM
1190 LOCATE 20,20:PRINT "ONLY 1,2 OR 3 PERMITTED, ENTER AGAIN":GOTO 1150
1200 REM ***********END OF MENU PROGRAM ************************
1210 PRINT "SERIES CONVERSION TO "
```

```
1220 PRINT "CONTINUE ?, Y OR N";:INPUT ANSWER$
1230 IF ANSWER$="n" THEN LET ANSWER$="N"
1240 IF ANSWER$="N" THEN GOTO 1080
1250 IF ANSWER$ ="y" THEN LET ANSWER$="Y"
1260 IF ANSWER$ "Y" THEN PRINT "ONLY Y OR N ALLOWED, RE-ENTER"
1270 IF ANSWER$ "Y" THEN GOTO 1210
1280 REM ***************************************** *****************
1290 REM  IDENTIFIES SERIES TO BE ACCESSED
1300 REM ***************************************** *****************
1310 PRINT "SERIES CODE TITLE MUST BE ENTERED";:INPUT;FILENO$
1320 REM THE VAL COMMAND CONVERTS A STRING TO A NUMBER
1330 IF VAL(MID$(FILENO$,4,3))=J THEN LET FILENAME$="BCIHIST1.DAT"
1340 IF VAL(MID$(FILENO$,4,3))=75 AND VAL(MID$(FILENO$,4,3))=C THEN LET
FILENAME$="BCIHIST2.DAT"
1350 IF VAL(MID$(FILENO$,4,3))=324 AND VAL(MID$(FILENO$,4,3))= THEN LET
FILENAME$="BCIHIST3.DAT"
1360 IF VAL(MID$(FILENO$,4,3))=739 THEN LET FILENAME$="BCIHIST4.DAT"
1370 OPEN FILENAME$ FOR INPUT AS #1 'OPENS DISK FILE TO ACCESS INFOR-
MATION
1380 INPUT #1, RECORD$ 'INPUTS A RECORD FROM THE FILE OPENED
1390 IF EOF(1) THEN GOTO 2470 'IF NO FILE FOUND GOES TO ERROR MESSAGE
1400 IF LEFT$(RECORD$,6)=FILENO$ THEN PRINT RECORD$ ELSE GOTO 1380
1410 LET SERIES.TITLE$=MID$(RECORD$,8,112)
1420 LET SERIES.NO$=MID$(RECORD$,4,3)
1430 LET SERIES.TOT$=LEFT$(RECORD$,6)
 1440 INPUT #1, RECORD$
1450 IF LEFT$(RECORD$,6)  SERIES.TOT$ THEN INPUT#1,RECORD$
1460 IF LEFT$(RECORD$,6)  SERIES.TOT$ THEN INPUT #1, RECORD$
1470 LET BEGIN%=VAL(MID$(RECORD$,23,2))
1480 LET YR.BEGIN%=1900+BEGIN%
1490 LET MO.BEGIN%=VAL(MID$(RECORD$,21,2))
1500 LET Y.END%=VAL(MID$(RECORD$,27,2))
1510 LET YR.END%=1900+Y.END%
1520 LET MO.END%=VAL(MID$(RECORD$,25,2))
1530 PRINT SERIES.TOT$, SERIES.NO$, SERIES.TITLE$,MO.BEGIN%,YR.BEGIN%,
MO.END%,YR.END%
1540 LET HFILE$=SERIES.NO$
1550 OPEN HFILE$ FOR OUTPUT AS #3
1560 WRITE #3, SERIES.TOT$,SERIES.NO$,SERIES.TITLE$,MO.BEGIN %,YR.BE-
GIN%,MO.END%,YR.END%
1570 CLOSE #3
1580 LET PERIOD%=VAL(MID$(RECORD$,29,2))
1590 IF PERIOD%=1 THEN LET PERIODS%=12
1600 IF PERIOD%=3 THEN LET PERIOD%=4
1610 LET NEW.FILENAME$=SERIES.NO$+".TSP"
1620 OPEN NEW.FILENAME$ FOR OUTPUT AS #2
1630 IF LEFT$(RECORD$,6)=SERIES.TOT$ THEN INPUT #1, RECORD$
1640 IF LEFT$(RECORD$,6)  SERIES.TOT$ THEN INPUT #1,RECORD$
```

```
1650 IF LEFT$(RECORD$,6)SERIES.TOT$ THEN CLOSE:GOTO 1210
1660 IF PERIOD%=4 THEN GOTO 1810
1670 REM ********************************************* ***************
1680 REM FOR MONTHLY DATA CONVERSION-CHOICE #1 FROM ABOVE
1690 REM ********************************************* ***************
1700 LET Z=8 'SETS UP A COUNTER TO READ THE FORMAT IN 1420
 1710 FOR X=1 TO 12
1720 LET A#(X)=VAL(MID$(RECORD$,Z,10))
1730 LET Z=Z+10
1740 IF X=12 THEN WRITE #2, A#(1),A#(2),A#(3),A#(4),A#(5),A#(6),A#(7),A#(
8),A#(9),A#(10),A#(11),A#(12)
1750 NEXT X
1760 GOTO 1630
1770 END
1780 REM ********************************************* ***************
1790 REM   FOR QUARTERLY DATA CONVERSION
1800 REM ********************************************* ***************
1810 LET Z=28
1820 FOR X=1 TO 4
1830 LET A#(X)=VAL(MID$(RECORD$,Z,10))
1840 LET Z=Z+30
1850 IF X=4 THEN WRITE #2, A#(1), A#(2), A#(3), A#(4)
1860 NEXT X
1870 GOTO 1630
1880 REM END OF PROGRAM CREATING CONVERTED FILE-CHOICE #1 **
1890 REM ********************************************* ***************
1900 REM PRINTOUT OF SERIES-CHOICE #2 FROM ABOVE
1910 REM ********************************************* ***************
1920 PRINT "SET PAPER TO TOP OF FORM"
1930 ON ERROR GOTO 2470
1940 LPRINT CHR$(27) CHR$(67) CHR$(66)
1950 LPRINT CHR$(27) CHR$(78) CHR$(6)
1960 PRINT "WHAT IS SERIES DESIRED TO BE PRINTED ";:INPUT SERIES$
1970 IF LEN(SERIES$)=1 THEN LET HSERIES$="00"+SERIES$
1980 IF LEN(SERIES$)=2 THEN LET HSERIES$="0"+SERIES$
1990 IF LEN(SERIES$)=3 THEN LET HSERIES$=SERIES$
2000 IF LEN(SERIES$)=1 THEN SERIES$="00"+SERIES$+"."
2010 IF LEN(SERIES$)=2 THEN LET SERIES$="0"+SERIES$+"."
2020 IF LEN(SERIES$)=3 THEN LET SERIES$=SERIES$+"."
2030 PRINT "PRINTING SERIES ";SERIES$
2040 LET PRINTFILE$=SERIES$
2050 LET HEADERFILE$=HSERIES$
2060 OPEN PRINTFILE$ FOR INPUT AS #1
2070 OPEN HEADERFILE$ FOR INPUT AS #2
2080 INPUT #2, SERIES.TOT$,SERIES.NO$,SERIES.TITLE$,MO.BEGIN %,YR.BE-
GIN%,MO.END%, YR.END%
2090 LET PERIOD$=MID$(SERIES.TOT$,3,1)
```

```
2100 LET PRINT.YEARS=(YR.END%-YR.BEGIN%)+1
2110 LET J=PRINT.YEARS
2120 IF PERIOD$="Q" THEN GOTO 2330
2130 REM ************************************** ****************
2140 REM PRINTS MONTHLY SERIES-CHOICE #2 FROM ABOVE
2150 REM ************************************** ****************
2160 FOR A=1 TO J 'SETS UP NUMBER OF YEARS TO PRINT OUT
2170 IF A=1 THEN LPRINT SERIES.TOT$, SERIES.NO$, SERIES.TITLE$,MO.BEGIN%;"
";YR.BEGIN%, MO.END%;" ";YR.END%
2180 IF A 1 THEN LET YR.BEGIN%=YR.BEGIN%+1
2190 INPUT #1, A#(1),A#(2),A#(3),A#(4),A#(5),A#(6),A#(7),A#(
8),A#(9),A#(10),A#(11),A#(12)
2200 LET W=15
2210 FOR Y=1 TO 12
2220  IF Y=7 THEN LET W=15
2230  IF Y=1 OR Y=7 THEN LPRINT TAB(5) YR.BEGIN%;
2240  LPRINT TAB(W) A#(Y);
2250  LET W=W+10
2260 NEXT Y
2270 NEXT A
2280 LPRINT CHR$(12) 'GOES TO TOP OF FORM AND CLEARS PRINTER
2290 CLOSE:GOTO 1080
2300 REM ************************************** ****************
2310 REM   PRINTS QUARTERLY SERIES
2320 REM ************************************** ****************
2330 FOR A=1 TO J
2340 IF A=1 THEN LPRINT SERIES.TOT$, SERIES.NO$, SERIES.TITLE$,MO.BEGIN%;"
";YR.BEGIN%, MO.END%;" ";YR.END%
2350 IF A 1 THEN LET YR.BEGIN%=YR.BEGIN%+1
2360  INPUT #1,A#(1),A#(2),A#(3),A#(4)
2370 LET W=15
2380 FOR Y=1 TO 4
2390  IF Y=1 THEN LPRINT TAB(5) YR.BEGIN%;
2400  LPRINT TAB(W) A#(Y);
2410  LET W=W+10
2420 NEXT Y
2430 NEXT A
2440 LPRINT CHR$(12)
2450 CLOSE:GOTO 1080
2460 REM *************************************************************
2470 PRINT "NO SUCH SERIES IS AVAILABLE, PLEASE RE-ENTER":FOR X=1 TO
15000: NEXT X:CLOSE:GOTO 1080
2480 REM ************************************** ****************
2490 REM *******************END OF PROGRAM*********************
2500 REM ************************************** ****************
```

To use the program, enter the lines exactly, using GWBASIC, BA-SICA, or a word processor in nondocument mode. Save the program entered under a filename of eight characters or less, such as "convert." Then transfer the program to the directory containing the data, using the COPY command.

On starting the program, GWBASIC must be present. After the BA-SIC language program is loaded, the program is loaded using the LOAD "Filename" command. After an "ok" appears on the screen, enter RUN. Thereafter, the program is menu driven. If any problems are encountered, simply press the CONTROL and BREAK keys, enter CLOSE to close all open files, and then enter RUN.

On completing the conversion, a printed copy is available by menu choice. This program supplies an extension to the series of TSP. (See Line 1610 in Program). This extension was added to facilitate copying the files to the other programs desired. To copy the files to another directory, such as a statistical program, one only needs to enter COPY *.TSP, and all the files that one creates with this program would be copied. After copying, the files can be deleted using just ERASE *.TSP, and disk space will be restored.

The need for specialized programs to convert does not arise very often; but if one is using disks or tapes supplied by others, the format may differ from that needed by the user.

STATISTICAL PROGRAMS

Software provides the instructions necessary for the computer to analyze a time series. After the data are available in a format acceptable to a software program, it is processed. A large number of statistical programs are available which provide the user with this processing power. Several programs of general use include:

SPSS	SPSS Inc. 444 Michigan Avenue, Chicago, Illinois
MICRO TSP	Quantitative Micro Software 4521 Campus Drive, Suite 336 Irvine, California

SAS   SAS Institute, Inc.
                       SAS Campus Drive,
                       Cary, North Carolina

All of the above software packages are supported by manuals, which include instructions on the use of the programs on the computer and a description of the statistical procedures employed.

PART II

LEADING INDICATORS

CHAPTER 4

INTRODUCTION

Leading indicators are defined by the Bureau of Economic Analysis as those indicators that are most capable of predicting peaks and troughs of business cycles in advance.

The importance of leading indicators arises out of their signals as to what might be possible in the future. Possibility does not mean certainty. If a leading indicator's action is confirmed by the action of other indicators, the level of assurance is increased. Since the purpose of a leading indicator is to supply advance warning, intervention by government action may take place. Illustrative of this action is the 1991 response by the Federal Reserve Board in decreasing interest rates. This intervention could prolong or decrease the length of any expansion or contraction phase. After leading indicators signal the possible change in trend, a recession or recovery might not take place. This would seem to cast doubt on the predictive value of the leading indicators. The purpose is advance warning. Intervention can change the outcome because of actions commenced because of reliance upon these same leading indicators.

There is not one but many leading indicators that are evaluated. Some are more successful in the advance prediction of peaks, while others call the turns at troughs. A cross section of indicators from many different areas of economic activity is needed, so that the extent of diffusion throughout the economy may be observed. The relevancy of indicators may change over time as other indicators are developed, or budget considerations may require less coverage. The number of indicators evaluated as leading are listed by economic process and their subprocess in the chart below. Shown in parentheses, if different, is the present number of series reproduced and supported by the BEA, as contrasted to the number reviewed and classified as leading in the *Handbook of Cyclical Indicators* in 1984.

CYCLICAL LEADING INDICATORS		
	NUMBER OF SERIES EVALUATED AT	
	PEAKS	THROUGHS
I. Employment and Unemployment		
a. Marginal Employment Adjustments	3	1
b. Job Vacancies	2	
c. Comprehensive Employment	1	
d. Comprehensive Unemployment	3	
II. Production and Income		
a. Capacity Utilization	2	
b. Industrial Production		1
III. Consumption, Trade, Order, and Delivery		
a. Orders and Deliveries	6 (4)	5 (4)
b. Consumption and Trade	2 (3)	4 (5)
IV. Fixed Capital Investment		
a. Formation and Business Enterprises	2	2
b. Business Investment Commitments	5 (4)	4 (3)
c. Residential Construction	3	3
V. Inventories and Inventory Investment		
a. Inventory Investment	4 (2)	4 (2)
b. Inventories on Hand and on Order	1 (0)	
VI. Prices, Costs, and Profits		
a. Stock Prices	1	1
b. Sensitive Commodity Prices	2 (3)	3 (3)
c. Profits and Profit Margins	7 (4)	6 (5)
d. Cash Flows	2 (1)	2 (1)
VII. Money and Credit		
a. Money	5 (4)	4 (3)
b. Credit Flows	5 (4)	5 (4)
c. Credit Difficulties	2	2
d. Bank Reserves	2	
e. Interest Rates	1	

PRESENTING THE INDIVIDUAL SERIES

Certain abbreviations are used in the presentation of the individual indicators and measures. These abbreviations have been adopted for use by
the BEA and appear in the *Survey of Current Business* and other publications.

To describe the procedures used, the following individual series is
presented as a sample.

**Average Weekly Hours of Production of Nonsupervisory Work-
ers—Manufacturing (1) (M,3) (L,L,L).** The title of the series is descriptive
of its makeup. Average weekly hours can be less than scheduled hours
because of absenteeism, labor turnover, part-time work, and shortages,
while overtime would cause weekly hours to be higher.

Exhibit 4-1

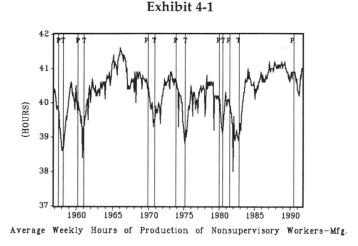

Average Weekly Hours of Production of Nonsupervisory Workers–Mfg.

From the above:

The series title is listed first.

**Average Weekly Hours of Production of Nonsupervisory Workers—
Manufacturing**

Next is the series number, which is used by the BEA: **(1)**, which is fol-
lowed by **(M,3)** for the type of indicator, monthly **M**, or quarterly **Q**, and
the source of the time series.

As part of the description of any indicator or measure, certain abbreviations are used for the sources of the information. These abbreviations are as follows:

1 — U.S. Department of Commerce, Bureau of Economic Analysis

2 — U.S. Department of Commerce, Bureau of the Census

3 — U.S. Department of Labor, Bureau of Labor Statistics

4 — Board of Governors of the Federal Reserve

Sources other than the above are identified as noted following the type of indicator. In this instance, the U. S. Department of Labor, Bureau of Labor Statistics, was identified as the source by using the **3** as a code.

Following the source is **(L,L,L)** or any combination of abbreviations, that identifies the indicator as **L** for Leading, **C** for Coincident, **Lg** for Lagging, and **U** for Unclassified. The first of the three descriptors is the timing at peaks, the next at troughs, and the last at all turns.

The definition of the series is next.

The title of the series is descriptive of its makeup. Average weekly hours can be less than scheduled hours because of absenteeism, labor turnover, part-time work, and shortages, while overtime would cause weekly hours to be higher.

These definitions are from the Department of Commerce, Bureau of Commerce, publication, *Handbook of Cyclical Indicators*, (1984). Where possible, the exact definition is used, except where a base year change has taken place, or the definition has been shortened.

After the definition, a graph of the time series is displayed.

Exhibit 4-2

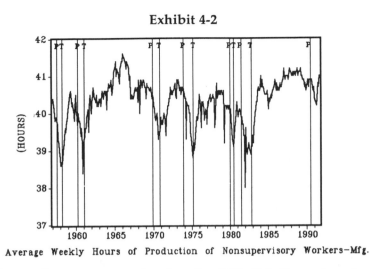

Average Weekly Hours of Production of Nonsupervisory Workers—Mfg.

This graph was prepared using the BCI diskette series, described previously, and data supplied by the BEA through the National Income and Product department. Missing data was accessed through the Citibase or Haver Analytics databases. In certain cases, the datasets were shortened because of inadequate or inaccurate data.

Business cycle peaks are denoted by P and troughs by T on the graphs. These peak and trough dates conform to the dates established by the National Bureau of Economic Research and are more completely described in Table 1-1.

Statistics as to the particular indicator are from the Department of Commerce Handbook (1984) referred to above.

Additions and Deletions

All indicators included in the latest statistical studies of 1984 and categorized as leading indicators at either peaks coincident, or troughs are reproduced and described. Some of these indicators are not supported presently, in the sense that they are no longer reproduced because of

■ duplication by other indicators, i.e., a constant value is reproduced instead of a current value indicator. These types of indicators can be recaptured by maintaining an indicator with data collected from the Business Statistics Branch of the BEA. Many large data vendors may maintain the series also.

- loss of timeliness because so many different organizations, branches, etc. contributed to the indicator. These series are not reported and probably are not available from other sources.

- other indicators are added, replacing the indicators dropped. Statistical analysis is lacking for these indicators since they were added since the study.

Many of the indicators which are not presently supported or reproduced by the BEA may be available through the Business Statistics Branch of the BEA or through private vendors.

The older analysis is important because it gives effect to scoring of many more indicators than presently supported. Its inclusion provides an indication of indicators previously used and discarded in favor of others.

In November 1991, many indicators previously maintained with a base year of 1982 were changed to a base year of 1987. Most quarterly indicators or measures are part of the National Income and Product accounts, and now have a base year of 1987.

CHAPTER 5

EMPLOYMENT AND UNEMPLOYMENT

If unemployment is high, this could indicate a lack of sales necessary to maintain production levels. If sales are slackening, layoffs are a natural result. Overtime hours would also be decreased, and the lack of demand for labor would be reflected in an increase in claims for unemployment. A decrease of advertising help-wanted ads could also anticipate lessening production. These indicators are shown below.

SERIES	CATEGORY
Average Weekly Hours, Mfg.	Marginal Employment Adjustments
Average Weekly Overtime Hours, Mfg.	Marginal Employment Adjustments
Average Weekly Initial Claims (inverted)	Marginal Employment Adjustments
Ratio of Help-Wanted Advertising to Unemployment	Job Vacancies
Index of Help-Wanted Advertised in Newspaper	Job Vacancies
Employees on Non-Agricultural Payroll-Goods Producing Industries	Comprehensive Employment
Number of Persons Unemployed	Comprehensive Unemployment
Unemployment Rate (inverted)	Comprehensive Unemployment
Average Weekly Insured Unemployment Rate	Comprehensive Unemployment

MARGINAL EMPLOYMENT ADJUSTMENTS

DESCRIPTION/DEFINITION

Three indicators deal with production activity in hours and unemployment claims.

Average Weekly Hours of Production of Nonsupervisory Workers—Manufacturing (1) (M,3) (L,L,L). The title of the series is descriptive of its makeup. Average weekly hours can be less than scheduled hours because of absenteeism, labor turnover, part-time work, and shortages, while overtime would cause weekly hours to be higher.

Exhibit 5-1

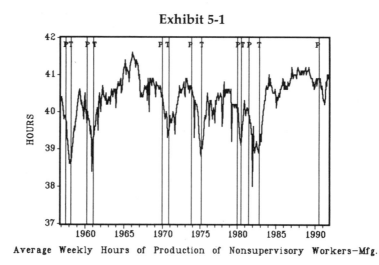

Average Weekly Hours of Production of Nonsupervisory Workers—Mfg.

Notice the lower weekly hours at troughs as contrasted to the increase during expansion phases of the economy. This is the only marginal employment adjustment indicator that is leading at both peaks and troughs.

Average Weekly Overtime Hours of Production or Nonsupervisory Workers—Manufacturing (21) (M,3) (L,C,L) measures hours for which overtime compensation is received. Shift differentials, hazard, or other incentive pay is excluded.

Exhibit 5-2

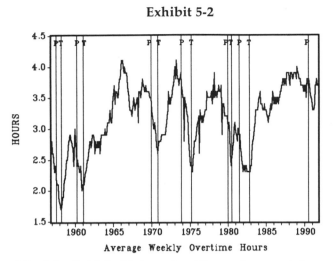

Average Weekly Overtime Hours

Average Weekly Initial Claims for Unemployment Insurance, State Programs (5) (M,U.S. Department of Labor, Employment and Training Administration; seasonal adjustment by Bureau of Economic Analysis) (L,C,L). Over 97 percent of wage and salary workers are covered by unemployment insurance. Unemployment claims are adjusted so that the series refers to the week in which the claim appears.

Exhibit 5-3

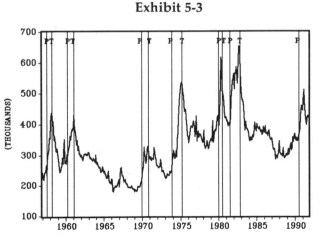

Average Weekly Initial Claims for Unemployment Insurance, State Programs

SIGNIFICANCE

Hours worked as well as overtime hours would be indicators of how tight the production schedules are in the manufacturing area. The average weekly claims give additional information as to the effects of operating at more or fewer hours of overall employment.

Production activity should be a function of hours worked. Also capacity utilization would seem to be a good proxy for hours worked.

SERIES	PEAK (in months)		TROUGH (in months)	
	Mean	Standard Deviation	Mean	Standard Deviation
Average Weekly Hours	-11.0	5.2	-1.6	2.0
Average Weekly Overtime Hours	-14.0	5.3	NA	NA
Average Weekly claims	-14.7	5.3	NA	NA

JOB VACANCIES

DESCRIPTION/DEFINITION

There are two series, one a ratio and the other an index using help-wanted advertising as a gauge of the tightness of the labor market.

Ratio, Help-Wanted Advertising in Newspapers to Number of Persons Unemployed (60) (M,1,3, and The Conference Board) (L,Lg,U). This is a ratio computed by dividing the Index of Help-Wanted Advertising by the Number of Persons Unemployed with an index of 1967=100 base.

Exhibit 5-4

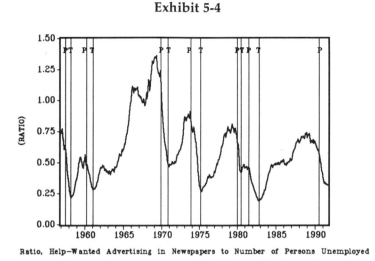

Ratio, Help—Wanted Advertising in Newspapers to Number of Persons Unemployed

Index of Help-Wanted Advertising in Newspapers (46) (M, The Conference Board) (L,Lg,U) is an index based upon the daily volume of help-wanted ads published in the classified section of one newspaper in each of 51 sample cities, which represent major labor markets.

Exhibit 5-5

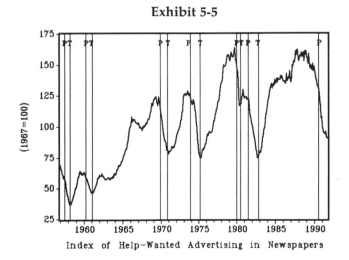

Index of Help—Wanted Advertising in Newspapers

SIGNIFICANCE

As classified ads increase, it becomes apparent that a tightness for labor exists and vice-versa. The degree of space variation between periods of labor plenty and shortage can be shown by comparing this series to series 21, representing overtime hours.

STATISTICS

SERIES	PEAK (in months)	
	Mean	Standard Deviation
Ratio-Help Wanted	-8.0	4.2
Index of Help Wanted	-8.7	5.8

COMPREHENSIVE EMPLOYMENT

DESCRIPTION/DEFINITION

A measurement of employed personnel can be found in the manufacturing, mining, and construction industries.

Employees on Nonagricultural Payroll, Goods-Producing Industries (40) (M,3) (L,C,U) measures the number of persons employed in mining, manufacturing, and construction industries.

Exhibit 5-6

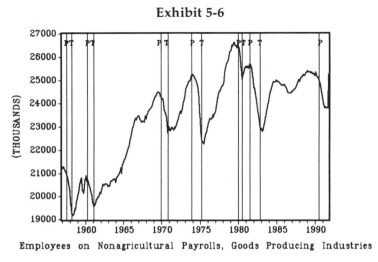

Employees on Nonagricultural Payrolls, Goods Producing Industries

SIGNIFICANCE

The total number of employees varies with each business cycle activity. A decrease in total numbers employed would cause one to believe that production is falling off, leading to increased unemployment and a decrease in output.

Since gross national product in current items has been growing, one would expect that the number of persons employed would be increasing and/or productivity increasing. Since the service-sector employment is growing, additional indicators would be needed to measure total employment.

STATISTICS

This is a leading indicator at peaks only.

PEAK (in months)	
Mean	Standard Deviation
-8.0	4.2
-8.7	5.8

COMPREHENSIVE UNEMPLOYMENT

DESCRIPTION/DEFINITION

The following are three leading indicators used as predictors of market peaks. They are some of the most widely quoted and politically charged indicators.

Number of Persons Unemployed (37) (M,3) (L,LG,U) is a series which includes persons who were available for work but did not work during the survey week. It is filtered to include people who made an effort to find work. Simply stated, as unemployment becomes greater, economic activity becomes less.

Exhibit 5-7

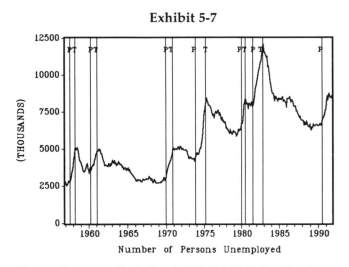

Number of Persons Unemployed

Civilian Unemployment Rate in % (43) (M,3) (L,Lg,U) is a measure derived from the ratio of the number of persons unemployed as a percent of the civilian labor force, which is inversely related to broad movements in aggregate economic activity.

Exhibit 5-8

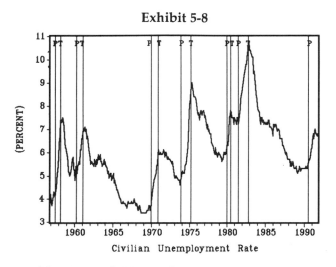

Civilian Unemployment Rate

Average Weekly Insured Unemployment Rate, State Programs (45) (M,U.S. Department of Labor, Employment and Training Administration) (L,Lg,U) is presented as a percent on an inverted scale. Insured employment measures the number of persons reporting approximately on the week of unemployment. It excludes people who have exhausted their benefit rights and workers who have not earned rights to unemployment insurance.

Exhibit 5-9

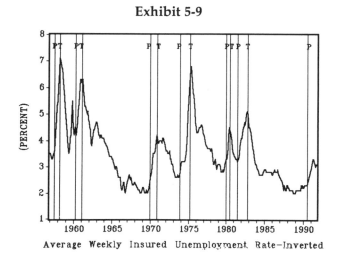

Average Weekly Insured Unemployment Rate–Inverted

SIGNIFICANCE

Unemployment provides important information on the level of economic activity. The unemployment rate is also an indicator which influences policies of government programs.

SERIES	PEAK (in months)	
	Mean	Standard Deviation
Number of Persons Unemployed	-5.7	4.0
Unemployment Rate in %	-4.9	3.4
Average Weekly Insured Unemployment Rate	-5.9	7.2

SERIES SCORES

Tables 5-1, 5-2, and 5-3 display the scores of the indicators, showing their performance at peak and trough dates. All series scores are from the Department of Commerce, Bureau of Economic Analysis Handbook (1984).

Table 5-1: Series Scores: Employment and Unemployment

| Series | Timing | | | Conformity | Smoothness | Currency | Statistical Adequacy | Economic Significance | Revisions | Total | | |
| | Peaks | Troughs | All Turns | | | | | | | Peaks | Troughs | All Turns |
	(1)	(2)	(3)	(4)	(5)	(6)	(7)	(8)	(9)	(10)	(11)	(12)
Marginal Employment Adjustments:												
1. Average Weekly Hours of Production or Nonsupervisory Workers, Mfg.	74	86	80	67	60	80	84	70	80	74	77	75
21. Average Weekly Overtime Hours of Production or Nonsupervisory Workers, Mfg.	63	82	64	85	60	80	79	60	80	71	76	72
*5. Average Weekly Initial Claims For Unemployment Insurance, State Programs (Inverted)	76	79	70	86	60	80	85	80	80	79	79	77
Job Vacancies:												
60. Ratio, Help-Wanted Advertising in Newspapers to Persons Unemployed	78	78	78	86	100	80	56	70	80	77	77	77
46. Index of Help-Wanted Advertising in Newspapers	75	86	81	86	100	80	47	70	80	75	78	77

* A component of a major composite index.

Table 5-2: Series Scores:Employment and Unemployment - Continued (1)

| Series | Timing | | | Conformity | Smoothness | Currency | Statistical Adequacy | Economic Significance | Revisions | Total | | |
	Peaks	Troughs	All Turns							Peaks	Troughs	All Turns
	(1)	(2)	(3)	(4)	(5)	(6)	(7)	(8)	(9)	(10)	(11)	(12)
Comprehensive Employment:												
48. Employee hours in Nonagricultural Establishments	9	78	92	83	80	80	84	90	40	61	78	82
42. Number of Persons Engaged in Nonagricultural Activities	11	80	84	78	80	80	64	90	100	64	81	82
*41. Employees on Nonagricultural Payrolls	79	97	96	82	100	80	84	90	60	82	87	87
40. Employees on Nonagricultural Payrolls, Goods-Producing Industries	42	92	96	84	100	80	84	80	60	72	84	85
90. Ratio, Civilian Employment to Population of Working Age	6	90	84	74	60	80	64	90	100	60	81	79

* A component of a major composite index.

Table 5-3: Series Scores: Employment and Unemployment - Continued (2)

Series	Timing			Conformity	Smoothness	Currency	Statistical Adequacy	Economic Significance	Revisions	Total		
	Peaks	Troughs	All Turns							Peaks	Troughs	All Turns
	(1)	(2)	(3)	(4)	(5)	(6)	(7)	(8)	(9)	(10)	(11)	(12)
Comprehensive Unemployment:												
37. Number of Persons Unemployed (Inverted)	79	83	81	93	80	80	64	90	100	83	84	83
43. Unemployment Rate (Inverted)	80	87	84	100	80	80	64	90	100	84	86	85
45. Average Weekly Insured Unemployment Rate, State Programs (Inverted)	33	90	84	79	100	80	84	80	80	71	85	83
*91. Average Duration of Unemployment in Weeks (Inverted)	74	91	89	96	80	80	64	90	100	82	86	86
44. Unemployment Rate, Persons Unemployed 15 Weeks and Over (Inverted)	91	83	89	100	80	80	64	80	100	85	83	85

* A component of a major composite index.

CHAPTER 6

PRODUCTION AND INCOME

Production cannot increase indefinitely. A point is reached beyond which present capacity cannot be stretched. Three of the indicators in the production and income areas measure this situation and are aptly termed capacity utilization. As utilization of capacity increases, so should the demand for labor and materials. This increase is reflected in increased costs to firms, individuals, and government. The leading indicators for this economic process are shown as follows:

SERIES	CATEGORY
Capacity Utilization Rate, Mfg.	Capacity Utilization
Capacity Utilization Rate, Materials*	Capacity Utilization
Capacity Utilization Rate, Total Industry	Capacity Utilization
Industrial Production, Nondurable Manufacturers	Industrial Production

*No longer reproduced by BEA.

THE INDIVIDUAL SERIES

In the discussion of the individual series, one notices that there are three leading peak indicators for this economic process. Other indicators in other economic processes may supply the same sort of information. For instance, average weekly hours of production of nonsupervisory workers in manufacturing would seem to be a good indicator for capacity utilization, as additional hours are needed when capacity increases.

CAPACITY UTILIZATION

DESCRIPTION/DEFINITION

Three rates, expressed in percent that actual output is at capacity output, are discussed. Capacity output is defined as the output level that can be achieved during a given period with existing plant and equipment and a normal operating schedule. The data is seasonally adjusted.

Capacity Utilization Rate—Manufacturing (82) (M,4) (L,C,U) is a derived measure of capacity utilization. The data sets used to estimate capacity by industry include:

1. The Board of Governors of the Federal Reserve System (FRB) industrial production indexes.

2. Surveys of manufacturers' utilization rates from McGraw-Hill Information Systems Company and the U.S. Department of Commerce, Bureau of the Census and BEA.

3. Gross capital stock estimates.

4. The McGraw-Hill survey of industrial capacity growth.

5. Capacity estimates in physical units from business and trade associations.

Exhibit 6-1

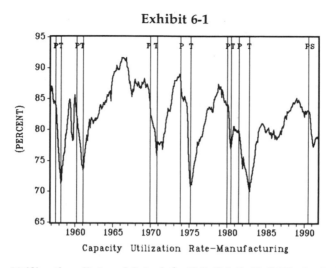

Capacity Utilization Rate—Manufacturing

Capacity Utilization Rate—Materials (84) (M,4) (L,C,U) is derived from weighted averages of output and capacity for each of the 96 material components of the FRB index of industrial production. The capacity series are based on the concept of "maximum practical output." Year-end capacity estimates are derived from the FRB indexes of industrial production and capacity utilization rates collected and published by trade associations, government agencies, and other sources.

Exhibit 6-2

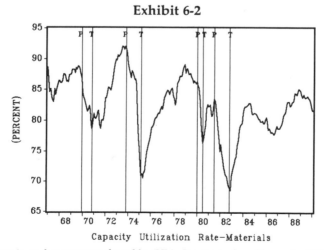

Capacity Utilization Rate—Materials

This indicator is no longer reproduced by BEA. It was replaced by series 124.

Capacity Utilization Rate—Total Industry (124) (M,L,C,U) is a rate for total industry as contrasted to that of just manufacturing.

Exhibit 6-3

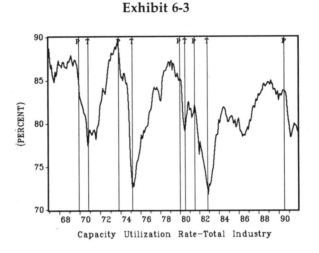

Capacity Utilization Rate—Total Industry

SIGNIFICANCE

Operation at maximum capacity would tend to support high employment, and marked decreases in the capacity utilization would make increases in unemployment likely. This indicator should be a predictor of unemployment and employment, since there would be a lag between actual layoff and an appearance in the employment statistics.

STATISTICS

SERIES	PEAK (in months)		TROUGH (in months)	
	Mean	Standard Deviation	Mean	Standard Deviation
Capacity Utilization Rate - Mfg.	-10.9	6.7	0.7	1.2
Capacity Utilization Rate - Mat.	-8.3	6.2	-0.6	2.3

INDUSTRIAL PRODUCTION

DESCRIPTION/DEFINITION

Index of Industrial Production, Nondurable Manufactures (74) (M,4) (C,L,L). This is an index that measures the production of the nondurable manufactured components of the industrial production index. Nondurable manufactures are those manufactured items with a normal life expectancy of less than three years. Foods, tobacco products, textile mill products, apparel products, paper products, printing and publishing, chemicals, petroleum products, rubber and plastic products, and leather products are included.

Exhibit 6-4

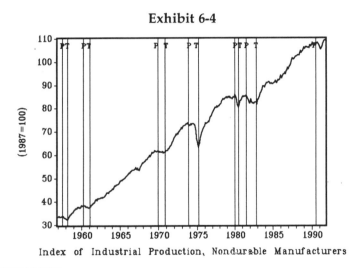

Index of Industrial Production, Nondurable Manufacturers

SIGNIFICANCE

This is a leading indicator of troughs. There are many other series available for industrial production, but their value as indicators has been that of coincident indicators.

STATISTICS

TROUGHS (in months)	
Mean	**Standard Deviation**
-2.0	2.2

SERIES SCORES

The series scores are shown in Table 6-1.

Table 6-1: Series Scores: Production and Income

Series	Timing					Statistical	Economic		Total		
	Peaks	Troughs	All Turns	Conformity	Smoothness	Currency	Adequacy	Significance	Revisions	Peaks	Troughs	All Turns
	(1)	(2)	(3)	(4)	(5)	(6)	(7)	(8)	(9)	(10)	(11)	(12)
Industrial Production												
74. Index of Industrial Production, Nondurable Manufacturers	72	65	85	78	100	80	77	80	40	75	74	79
Capacity Utilization:												
83. Capacity Utilization Rate, Mfg.	41	82	61	17	60	20	76	80	100	54	64	59
82. Capacity Utilization Rate, Manufacturers	73	96	76	71	80	20	67	80	60	67	73	68
84. Capacity Utilization Rate, Materials	74	89	82	72	80	20	52	70	60	64	67	66

* A component of a major composite index.

CHAPTER 7

CONSUMPTION, TRADE, ORDERS, AND DELIVERIES

Orders, deliveries, and sales could be expected to increase during expansion phases and decrease during contractions. A visual inspection of leading indicators in this economic process confirms our expectations.

These leading indicators are classified according to goods of a durable or nondurable nature. For example, one of the largest durable goods sold to individuals and firms is automobiles, while retail sales would involve items of a nondurable nature.

Several qualitative measures are also a part of this process. The series and categories included in this process follow, with series no longer reproduced by the BEA identified with an " * ".

SERIES	CATEGORY
Manufacturers' New Orders, Durable Goods*	Order and Deliveries
Manufacturers' New Orders in 1982 Dollars, Durable Goods	Order and Deliveries
Manufacturer's New Orders in 1982 Dollars, Consumer Goods and Materials	Order and Deliveries
Change in Manufacturers' Unfilled Orders, Durable Goods	Order and Deliveries
Manufacturer's Unfilled Orders, Durable Goods*	Order and Deliveries
Vendor Performance, Slower Delivery	Order and Deliveries
Index of Consumer Sentiment	Consumption and Trade
Index of Consumer Expectations	Consumption and Trade
Index of Consumer Confidence	Consumption and Trade
Index of Consumer Expectations	Consumption and Trade
Sales of Retail Stores in 1982 Dollars	Order and Deliveries
Sales of Retail Stores*	Order and Deliveries
Industrial Production, Consumer Goods	Order and Deliveries
Personal Consumption Expenditures Automobiles*	Order and Deliveries

ORDERS AND DELIVERIES

DESCRIPTION/DEFINITION

The following discusses six series of which all are leading indicators at peaks and five at troughs. All series are estimates of manufacturers' new or unfilled orders based on data collected in the monthly manufacturers' shipments, inventories and orders survey. The survey includes manufacturing companies with 1000 or more employees and selected small companies. New orders are intents to buy for immediate or future delivery and are supported by binding, legal documents. The series are seasonally adjusted.

Manufacturers' New Orders in Current Dollars, Durable Goods (6) (M,2) (L,L,L) measures the value of new orders of durable-goods manufacturers in current dollars.

Exhibit 7-1

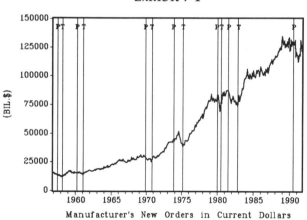

Manufacturer's New Orders in Current Dollars

No longer reproduced by BEA.

Manufacturers' New Orders in 1982 Dollars, Durable Goods Industries (7) (M,1 and 2) (L,L,L) is the series above deflated using the seasonally adjusted Producer Price Index.

Exhibit 7-2

Manufacturers' New Orders in 1982 Dollars, Durable Goods Industries

Manufacturers' New Orders in 1982 Dollars, Consumer Goods Industries and Material (8) (M,1 and 2) (L,L,L) includes durable-goods industries other than capital goods and defense producers and the four non-durable foods industries that have unfilled orders; namely, textile mill products, paper and allied products, printing, publishing and allied products, and leather products. Also, it is deflated by using the producer price indexes applicable to the 2-digit Standard Industrial Classification.

Exhibit 7-3

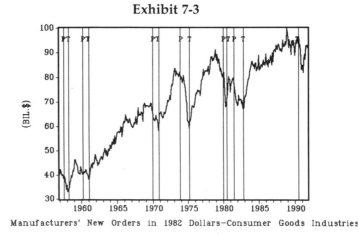

Manufacturers' New Orders in 1982 Dollars—Consumer Goods Industries

Manufacturers' Unfilled Orders, Durable Goods Industries (96) (EOM, 2) (L,Lg,U) measures the current dollar value of unfilled orders of durable goods. Manufacturers' durable goods are defined as those items with a normal life expectancy of three years or more.

Exhibit 7-4

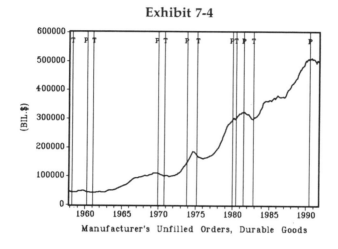

Manufacturer's Unfilled Orders, Durable Goods

No longer reproduced by BEA.

Change in Manufacturers' Unfilled Orders, Durable Goods Industries (25) (M,2) (L,L,L) reports the month-to-month amount of change in the series above.

Exhibit 7-5

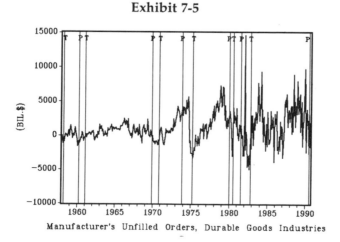

Manufacturer's Unfilled Orders, Durable Goods Industries

Vendor Performance, Slower Delivery (32) (M, National Association of Purchasing Management) (L,L,L) reflects a percentage of purchasing agents who experienced slower deliveries in the current month compared to the previous month. It tends to reflect the volume of business being handled by the suppliers of these firms, with slower deliveries usually due to a higher volume of business.

Exhibit 7-6

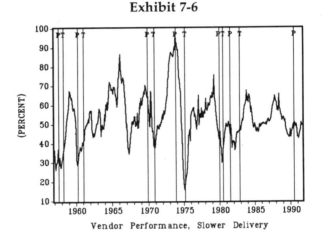

Vendor Performance, Slower Delivery

SIGNIFICANCE

All of these indicators are monthly indicators and could reflect events which could take place in the future. Unfilled orders would be converted to sales, etc. If unfilled orders were down, it could indicate a lessening of end-product demand.

STATISTICS

SERIES	PEAK (in months)		TROUGH (in months)	
	Mean	Standard Deviation	Mean	Standard Deviation
Manufacturers' New Orders, Durable Goods	-7.4	8.4	-1.4	1.3
Manufacturers' New Orders in 1982 Dollars, Durable Goods	-9.0	6.0	-1.1	1.4
Manufacturers' New Orders in 1982 Dollars, Consumer Goods &Material	-11.4	6.7	-2.0	2.4
Manufacturers' Unfilled Orders, Durable Goods	-5.7	9.4	NA	NA
Change in Manufacturers' Unfilled Orders, Durable Goods	-11.3	11.3	-5.0	4.1
Vendor Performance, Slower Deliveries	-9.0	6.2	-4.0	3.8

CONSUMPTION AND TRADE

DESCRIPTION/DEFINITION

There are several series, of which four deal primarily with sales and production while the others reflect consumer attitudes. All are series that
reflect consumer activity and/or perception.

**Index of Consumer Sentiment (58) (Q,M, University of Michigan, Sur-
vey Research Center) (L,L,L)** is a qualitative survey based upon five
questions, namely (1) an opinion on the financial condition of the re-
spondent and his family at present compared to a year earlier, (2) an
opinion on business conditions during the next 12 months, (4) during the
next 5 years, and (5) whether the present is a good time to purchase
consumer durables.

Exhibit 7-7

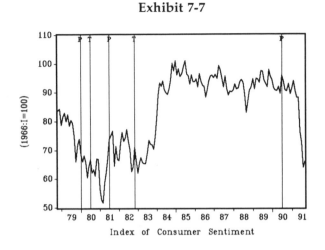

Index of Consumer Sentiment

Reproduced with permission of University of Michigan, Survey Research Center.

Index of Consumer Expectations (83) (M, University of Michigan Survey Research Center) (L,L,L)

Exhibit 7-8

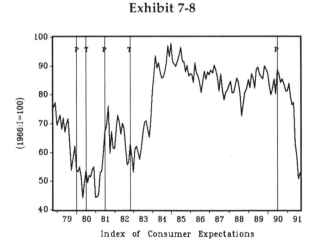

Index of Consumer Expectations

Reproduced with permission of University of Michigan, Survey Research Center.

Index of Consumer Confidence (122) (M, The Conference Board)

Exhibit 7-9

Index of Consumer Confidence

Index of Consumer Expectations (123) (M, The Conference Board)

Exhibit 7-10

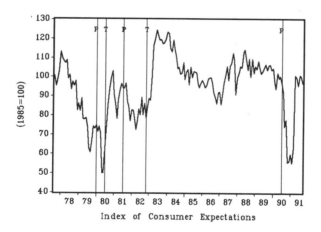

Index of Consumer Expectations

The Conference Board conducts a survey of approximately 5,000 persons. The differences in the indexes reflect varying questions in the surveys.

Sales of Retail Stores (54) (M,2) (C,L,U) measures net sales and receipts
to establishments primarily engaged in retail trade in current dollars. A
retail establishment is defined as one engaged primarily in selling merchandise for personal or household consumption. This series is adjusted
for holidays, trading days, and seasonal variations.

Exhibit 7-11

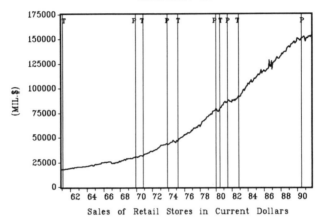

Sales of Retail Stores in Current Dollars

No longer reproduced by the BEA.

Sales of Retail Stores in 1982 Dollars (59) (M,1 and 2) (U,L,U) is the series above deflated using combinations of the Consumer Price Indexes.

Exhibit 7-12

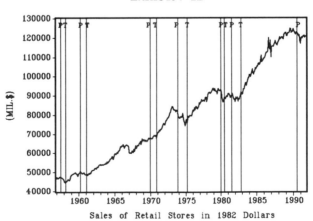

Sales of Retail Stores in 1982 Dollars

These series seem to confirm that the consumer does not spend as much when the outlook is not viewed favorably.

Index of Industrial Production—Consumer Goods (75) (M,4) (C,L,C) measures the production of the consumer goods components of the industrial production index. Consumer goods include automotive products and home goods in the durable-goods category and clothing and consumer staples in the nondurable-goods category. This index has a base of 1987=100.

Exhibit 7-13

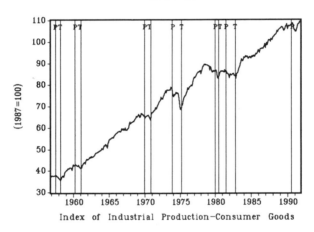

Index of Industrial Production–Consumer Goods

Personal Consumption Expenditures—Automobiles (55) (Q,10) (L,C,C) is a quarterly measure of consumer purchases of new cars and net purchases of used cars.

Exhibit 7-14

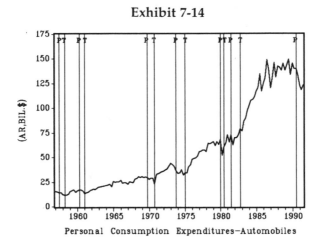

Personal Consumption Expenditures—Automobiles

No longer supported by the BEA.

SIGNIFICANCE

Sales in the consumer area should reflect both present and anticipated circumstances. If unemployment is high, one might expect that most of the indicators would represent a lessening of demand for consumer goods.

STATISTICS

SERIES	PEAK (in months)		TROUGH (in months)	
	Mean	Standard Deviation	Mean	Standard Deviation
Index of Consumer Sentiment	-15.2	11.3	-2.3	1.9
Sales of Retail Stores	NA	NA	-1.8	2.1
Sales of Retail Stores in 1982 Dollars	NA	NA	-1.6	2.1
Index of Industrial Production, Consumer Goods	NA	NA	-2.3	2.8
Personal Consumption Expenditures, Automobiles	-4.2	5.1	NA	NA

SERIES SCORES

Tables 7-1 and 7-2 provide information about the series scores.

Table 7-1: Series Scores: Consumption, Trade, Orders, and Deliveries

| Series | Timing | | | Conformity | Smoothness | Currency | Statistical Adequacy | Economic Significance | Revisions | Total | | |
| | Peaks | Troughs | All Turns | | | | | | | Peaks | Troughs | All Turns |
	(1)	(2)	(3)	(4)	(5)	(6)	(7)	(8)	(9)	(10)	(11)	(12)
Orders and Deliveries												
6. Manufacturers' New Orders in Current Dollars, Durable Goods industries	30	93	80	76	60	80	87	70	60	62	78	75
7. Manufacturers' New Orders in 1972 Dollars, Durable Goods Industries	62	89	84	76	60	80	87	70	60	70	77	76
*8. Manufacturers' New Orders in 1972 Dollars, Consumer Goods and Materials Industries	73	88	82	75	60	80	67	70	60	70	74	72
25. Change in Manufacturers' Unfilled Orders, Durable Goods Industries	27	84	79	26	40	80	87	70	60	52	66	65
96. Manufacturers' Unfilled Orders, Durable Goods Industries	2	68	65	87	100	80	87	70	60	61	78	77
*32. Vendor Performance, Percent of Companies Receiving Slower Deliveries	74	83	87	86	80	80	80	50	100	77	79	80

* A component of a major composite index.

Table 7-2: Series Scores: Consumption, Trade, Orders, and Deliveries - Continued

| Series | Timing | | | Conformity | Smoothness | Currency | Statistical Adequacy | Economic Significance | Revisions | Total | | |
| | Peaks | Troughs | All Turns | | | | | | | Peaks | Troughs | All Turns |
	(1)	(2)	(3)	(4)	(5)	(6)	(7)	(8)	(9)	(10)	(11)	(12)
Consumption and Trade:												
56. Mfg. and Trade Sales in Current Dollars	70	80	95	72	100	54	74	80	60	73	75	79
57. Mfg. and Trade Sales in 1972 Dollars	19	87	88	78	80	54	74	80	40	57	74	74
75. Index of Industrial Production, Consumer Goods	13	87	87	78	100	80	77	70	40	59	78	78
54. Sales of Retail Stores in Current Dollars	76	46	88	80	80	80	79	80	60	77	69	80
59. Sales of Retail Stores in 1972 Dollars	13	46	30	64	60	80	79	80	60	57	65	61
55. Personal Consumption Expenditures, Automobiles	10	44	27	69	40	20	94	50	60	46	55	51
58. Index of Consumer Sentiment	61	91	80	72	60	80	77	70	100	72	80	77

* A component of a major composite index.

CHAPTER 8

FIXED CAPITAL INVESTMENT

As new businesses are formed and older businesses expand, there is a need for additional plant and equipment. For the individual, the largest purchase of a lifetime is usually a house. All these activities take place during periods when they are affordable.

Generally, low interest rates make any project more feasible than it would be at a higher interest rate. For instance, an increase in long-term interest rates will cause many prospective home buyers to lose their ability to qualify because of increased mortgage payments. A projected plant addition may be feasible when money costs a certain amount, but when interest rates exceed that anticipated amount, the project is put on hold.

Government policies also influence fixed investment. Higher depreciation allowances, a lower service life, and investment tax credits are all examples of governmental intervention to influence fixed capital investment. The allowance of the interest deduction on personal income tax returns is also a method of making home ownership more desirable than renting.

Since many plans are put on hold because of high interest rates, one should expect that lower interest rates may cause a rapid increase in borrowings and an increase in investment in fixed capital.

All the leading indicators discussed have these following characteristics:

- Fixed investment peaks out and is then restarted at business troughs, and

- The reason for this is primarily because the business outlook is optimistic and interest rates are lower.

The series and categories of fixed capital investment are shown in the following chart:

SERIES	CATEGORY
Net Business Formation	Formation and Business Enterprises
New Business Incorporations	Formation and Business Enterprises
Contracts and Orders for Plant and Equipment	Business Investment and Commitments
Contracts and Orders for Plant and Equipment in 1982 Dollars	Business Investment and Commitments
Manufacturers' New Orders, Nondefense Capital Goods*	Business Investment and Commitments
Manufacturers' New Orders in 1982 Dollars, Nondefense Capital Goods	Business Investment and Commitments
Construction Contracts Awarded for Commercial and Industrial Buildings, Floor Space	Business Investment and Commitments
New Private Housing Units Started	Residential Construction
Index of New Private Housing Units	Residential Construction
Residential Fixed Investment in 1987 Dollars	Residential Construction

*No longer reproduced by the BEA.

FORMATION AND BUSINESS ENTERPRISE

DESCRIPTION/DEFINITION

Two indicators related to business formations.

Net Business Formation (12) (M,1; seasonal adjustment by Bureau of Economic Analysis and National Bureau of Economic Research, Inc.) (L,L,L) is an index with a 1967=100 base and is a monthly estimate of new formation of business enterprises. It is believed that this estimate adequately represents the short-term movement of new entries into and departures from the total business populations.

Exhibit 8-1

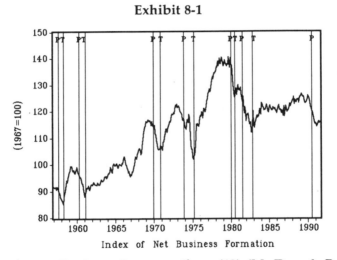

Index of Net Business Formation

Number of New Business Incorporations (13) (M, Dun & Bradstreet, Inc.; seasonal adjustment by Bureau of Economic Analysis and National Bureau of Economic Analysis) (L,L,L) measures the number of domestic stock profit companies receiving charters each month under the general business incorporation laws of the 50 states and the District of Columbia.

Exhibit 8-2

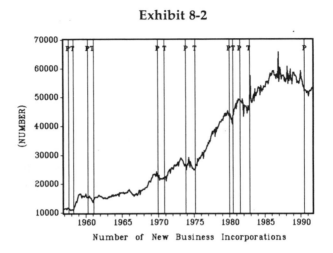

Number of New Business Incorporations

SIGNIFICANCE

As optimism and financing are available, new businesses are formed to take advantage of perceived opportunities, thus providing an indicator of public perception of the economic climate in periods ahead. In these cases, total net and number of new business formations should increase.

STATISTICS

These are both leading indicators for peaks and troughs.

SERIES	PEAK (in months)		TROUGH (in months)	
	Mean	Standard Deviation	Mean	Standard Deviation
Net Business Formation	-13.0	6.0	-1.6	1.0
Number of New Business Incorporations	-10.8	7.4	-3.2	3.1

BUSINESS INVESTMENT COMMITMENT

DESCRIPTION/DEFINITION

Five series relevant to long-term investment in plant and equipment are discussed.

Contracts and Orders for Plant and Equipment (10) (M,1,2, and McGraw-Hill Information Systems Company; seasonal adjustment by Bureau of the Census and Bureau of Economic Analysis, Inc.) (L,L,L) represents the value of new contracts awarded to building, public works, and utilities contractors and of new orders for nondefense goods received by manufacturers in capital goods industries.

Exhibit 8-3

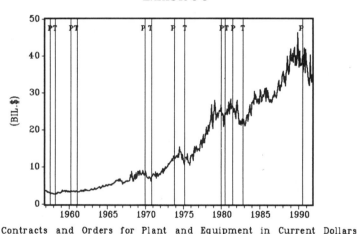

Contracts and Orders for Plant and Equipment in Current Dollars

Contracts and Orders of Plant and Equipment in 1982 Dollars (20) (M,1,2, McGraw-Hill Information Systems Company; seasonal adjustment by Bureau of the Census and Bureau of Economic Analysis, Inc.) (L,L,L) is the previous series deflated using applicable indexes.

Exhibit 8-4

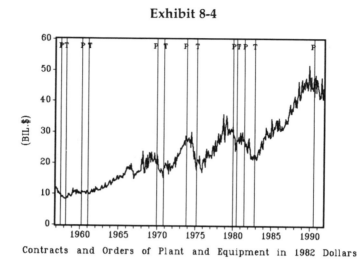

Contracts and Orders of Plant and Equipment in 1982 Dollars

Manufacturers' New Orders—Nondefense Capital Goods (24) (M,2) (L,L,L) is the sum of new orders received by capital goods and nondefense industries.

Exhibit 8-5

Manufacturer's New Orders—Nondefense Capital Goods

No longer reproduced by the BEA. The deflated series 27 is used as a proxy.

Manufacturers' New Orders in 1982 Dollars, Nondefense Capital Goods (27) (M,1 and 2) (L,L,L) is the previous series deflated using appropriate combinations of Producers Price Indexes.

Exhibit 8-6

Manufacturers' New Orders in 1982 Dollars, Nondefense Capital Goods

Construction Contracts Awarded for Commercial and Industrial Buildings (9) (M, McGraw-Hill Information Systems Company; seasonal adjustment by Bureau of the Census and Bureau of Economic Analysis) (L,C,U) measures the amount of floor space in both square footage and square meters specified in new contracts for work about to get underway on commercial buildings.

Exhibit 8-7

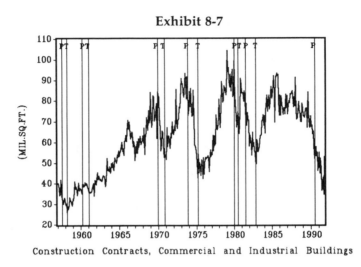

Construction Contracts, Commercial and Industrial Buildings

Reproduced with permission of McGraw-Hill Information Systems Company, F. W. Dodge Division.

SIGNIFICANCE

Long-term investment is one more indication of the future plans of American industry. If this investment is increasing, certain segments of the economy will surely benefit and vice-versa.

STATISTICS

SERIES	PEAK (in months)		TROUGH (in months)	
	Mean	Standard Deviation	Mean	Standard Deviation
Contracts and Orders for P&E	-5.0	6.3	-0.9	4.3
Contracts and Orders for P&E in 1982 Dollars	-5.0	6.3	-0.3	4.3
Manufacturers' New Orders, Non-defense Capital Goods	-9.7	10.1	-2.3	1.7
Manufacturers' New Orders in 1982 Dollars	-10.3	9.1	-2.3	1.7
Construction Contracts Awarded	-4.6	6.7	NA	NA

RESIDENTIAL CONSTRUCTION

DESCRIPTION/DEFINITION

The following are three series dealing with private housing units, which are defined as rooms meant for occupancy by a family or group of unrelated persons or by a person living alone. All transient accommodations are excluded.

New Private Housing Units Started (28) (M,2) (L,L,L) is   construction begun on a new building that is intended primarily as a housekeeping, residential building designed for nontransient occupancy.

Exhibit 8-8

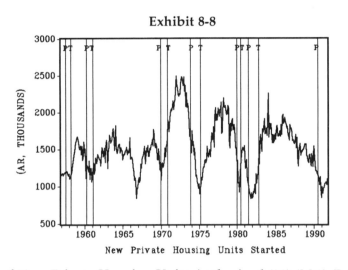

New Private Housing Units Started

Index of New Private Housing Units Authorized (29) (M,2) (L,L,L)
refers to permit issuance by local permit-issuing places. Predates the units started by a few months and may contain permits which have not started but are allowed to lapse.

Exhibit 8-9

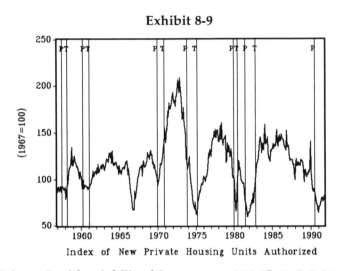

Index of New Private Housing Units Authorized

Gross Private Residential Fixed Investment (89) (Q,1) (L,L,L)
measures the value of domestic investment in residential structures in
constant (1987) dollars. The residential structures estimate is derived
from monthly data from private new construction of residential buildings compiled by the Census Bureau.

Exhibit 8-10

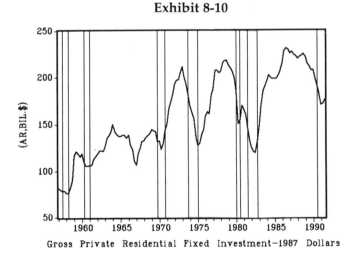

Gross Private Residential Fixed Investment—1987 Dollars

SIGNIFICANCE

Housing contributes greatly to the job market and to gross national product. Its contractions and expansions affect the supply and demand for labor which, in turn, affects consumer purchases. Housing activity is closely related to the level of interest rates.

STATISTICS

SERIES	PEAK (in months)		TROUGH (in months)	
	Mean	Standard Deviation	Mean	Standard Deviation
New Private Housing Units Started	-16.1	7.3	-4.9	3.6
Index of New Private Units	-15.3	6.9	-4.9	3.7
Gross Private Residential Fix Investment	-12.1	7.9	-3.1	2.5

SERIES SCORES

Series scores can be studied in Table 8-1 through Table 8-4.

Table 8-1: Series Scores: Fixed Capital Investment

Series	Timing			Conformity	Smoothness	Currency	Statistical Adequacy	Economic Significance	Revisions	Total		
	Peaks	Troughs	All Turns							Peaks	Troughs	All Turns
	(1)	(2)	(3)	(4)	(5)	(6)	(7)	(8)	(9)	(10)	(11)	(12)
Formation of Business Enterprises:												
*12. Index of Net Business Formation	73	96	82	70	80	80	70	70	40	70	76	72
13. Number of New Business Incorporations	32	82	78	68	60	27	75	70	80	57	69	68
Business Investment Commitments:												
10. Contracts and Orders for Plant and Equipment in Current Dollars	35	81	84	91	40	80	67	80	60	62	74	75
*20. Contracts and Orders for Plant and Equipment in 1972 Dollars	66	68	83	92	40	80	67	80	20	66	67	70

* A component of a major composite index.

Table 8-2: Series Scores: Fixed Capital Investment - Continued (1)

Series	Timing			Conformity	Smoothness	Currency	Statistical Adequacy	Economic Significance	Revisions	Total		
	Peaks	Troughs	All Turns							Peaks	Troughs	All Turns
	(1)	(2)	(3)	(4)	(5)	(6)	(7)	(8)	(9)	(10)	(11)	(12)
Business Investment Commitments - Continued												
24. Manufacturers' New Orders in Current Dollars, Nondefense Capital Goods Industries	27	93	79	85	60	80	72	70	60	61	77	74
27. Manufacturers' New Orders in 1972 Dollars, Nondefense Capital Goods Industries	27	93	79	85	40	80	72	70	60	59	76	72
9. Construction Contracts Awarded for Commercial and Industrial Buildings	7	56	31	78	20	80	95	70	100	58	70	64
11. Newly Approved Capital Appropriations, 1,000 Mfg. Corporations	67	72	79	82	60	20	85	70	80	68	70	71
97. Backlog of Capital Appropriations, 1,000 Mfg. Corporations	6	81	64	72	100	20	85	70	80	56	74	70

* A component of a major composite index.

Table 8-3: Series Scores: Fixed Capital Investment - Continued (2)

| Series | Timing | | | Conformity | Smoothness | Currency | Statistical Adequacy | Economic Significance | Revisions | Total | | |
| | Peaks | Troughs | All Turns | | | | | | | Peaks | Troughs | All Turns |
	(1)	(2)	(3)	(4)	(5)	(6)	(7)	(8)	(9)	(10)	(11)	(12)
Business Investment Expenditures:												
61. Expenditures for New Plant and Equipment by U.S. Nonfarm Business	70	65	89	60	100	20	87	80	100	73	72	78
69. Manufacturers' Machinery and Equipment Sales and Business Construction Expenditures	73	82	89	68	80	54	65	80	80	72	74	76
76. Index of Industrial Production, Business Equipment	11	92	93	82	100	80	77	70	40	59	79	80
86. Gross Private Nonresidential Fixed Investment in 1972 Dollars	91	91	100	72	80	20	87	80	60	75	75	77
87. Gross Private Nonresidential Fixed Investment in 1972 Dollars, Structures	8	81	78	67	80	20	87	70	60	52	70	69
88. Gross Private Nonresidential Fixed Investment in 1972 Dollars, Producers' Durable Equipment	72	91	96	67	80	20	87	70	60	68	72	74

* A component of a major composite index.

Table 8-4: Series Scores: Fixed Capital Investment - Continued (3)

Series	Timing			Conformity	Smoothness	Currency	Statistical Adequacy	Economic Significance	Revisions	Total		
	Peaks	Troughs	All Turns							Peaks	Troughs	All Turns
	(1)	(2)	(3)	(4)	(5)	(6)	(7)	(8)	(9)	(10)	(11)	(12)
Residential Construction Commitments and Investment:												
28. New Private Housing Units	72	86	80	39	60	80	85	80	60	69	72	71
*29. Index of New Private Housing Units Authorized by Local Building Permits	73	85	80	76	60	80	67	80	100	76	79	78
89. Gross Private Residential Fixed Investment in 1972 Dollars	71	88	80	68	80	20	87	80	60	69	73	71

* A component of a major composite index.

CHAPTER 9

INVENTORIES AND INVENTORY INVESTMENT

The expansion phase of a business cycle requires inventory to sustain that expansion. Since the expansion phase results in greater sales, inventories must be increased and maintained at a higher level than at a previous lower point in sales. As sales increases are not sustained, these levels will drop, resulting in consumption of present inventories to meet sales and also a lower investment in inventories because of lower sales.

Leading indicators for this economic process are as follows:

SERIES	CATEGORY
Change in Business Inventories in 1987 Dollars	Inventory Investment
Change in Mfg. and Trade Inventories on Hand and on Order in 1982 Dollars (smoothed)*	Inventory Investment
Change in Mfg. and Trade Inventories	Inventory Investment
Change in Manufacturers' Inventories, Materials and Supplies on Hand and on Order, Book Value*	Inventory Investment
Manufacturers' Inventories, Materials and Supplies on Hand and on Order*	Inventories on Hand and on Order

* No longer reproduced by BEA.

117

INVENTORY INVESTMENT

DESCRIPTION/DEFINITION

Four different series which represent changes in inventories on a current or constant 1987 dollar basis are discussed.

Change in Business Inventories in 1987 Dollars (30) (Q,1) (L,L,L) measures the quarter-to-quarter amount of change in the physical volume of inventories valued at the average price for the base period estimates in 1987. Business inventories include farm and nonfarm inventories. Nonfarm inventories include purchased materials, supplies, goods in process, finished goods, and goods purchased for resale. Farm inventories include livestock and harvested crops.

Exhibit 9-1

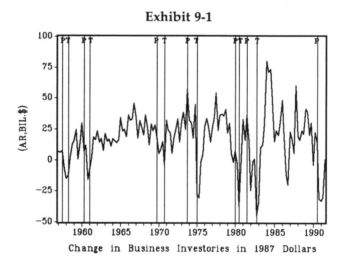

Change in Business Investories in 1987 Dollars

Change in Manufacturing and Trade Inventories on Hand and on Order in 1982 Dollars (36) (M,1 and 2) (L,L,L) reflects the month-to-month change in constant dollars. The appropriate producers price index is used as a deflator for this series.

Exhibit 9-2

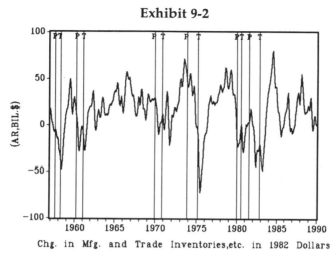

Chg. in Mfg. and Trade Inventories,etc. in 1982 Dollars

* No longer reproduced by BEA.

Change in Manufacturing and Trade Inventories (31) (M,1 and 2) (L,L,L) portrays the month-to-month change in inventories held by manufacturing, merchant wholesalers, and retail establishments at book value.

Exhibit 9-3

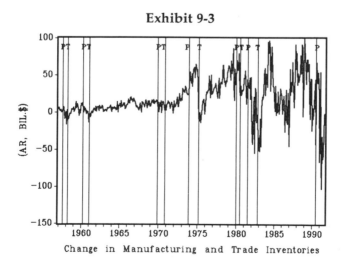

Change in Manufacturing and Trade Inventories

Change in Manufacturers' Inventories, Materials and Supplies on Hand and on Order (38) (M,2) (L,L,L) measures the change in value of manufacturers' materials and supplies inventories plus their unfilled orders for construction and other materials and supplies.

Exhibit 9-4

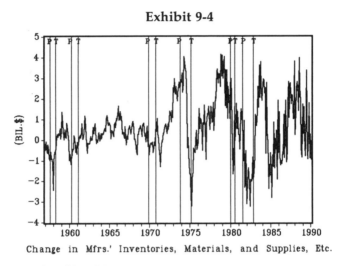

Change in Mfrs.' Inventories, Materials, and Supplies, Etc.

No longer reproduced by BEA.

SIGNIFICANCE

All of these indicators are classified as leading indicators at both peaks and troughs.

STATISTICS

SERIES	PEAK (in months)		TROUGH (in months)	
	Mean	Standard Deviation	Mean	Standard Deviation
Change in Business Inventories in 1982 Dollars	-8.3	8.0	-1.4	2.3
Change in Mfg. & Trade on Hand and on Order in 1982 Dollars	-10.1	5.1	-2.4	3.3
Change in MFG. Trade Inventories	4.4	7.2	-2.1	2.9
Change in Mfg. Inventories, Material and Supplies on Hand and on Order	-8.2	8.5	-5.5	4.4

INVENTORIES ON HAND AND ON ORDER

DESCRIPTION/DEFINITION

Manufacturers' Inventories, Materials and Supplies on Hand and on Order (78) (EOM,2) (L,Lg,Lg). is the value of manufacturers' materials and supplies inventories plus their unfilled orders for construction and other materials and supplies. Manufacturers' unfilled orders are shown in the dollar value of orders received but not yet invoiced.

Exhibit 9-5

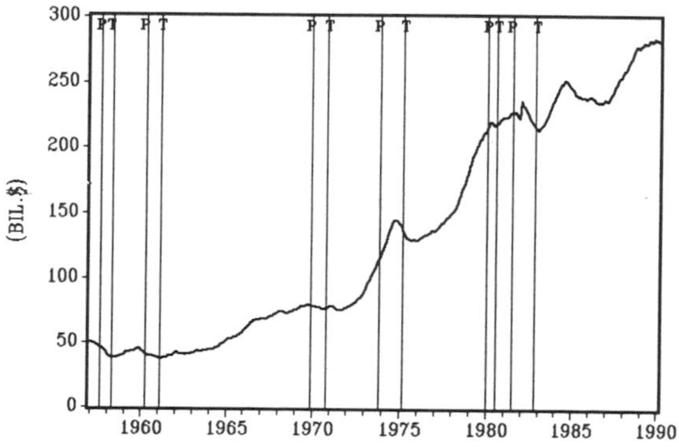

Mfrs. Inventories, Materials and Supplies on Hand and on Order

No longer reproduced by BEA.

SIGNIFICANCE

This value should and does increase over time as gross national product increases. The indicator is unadjusted for inflation. To sustain any expansion, larger inventories of materials and supplies are needed. A decrease could also reflect manufacturers' expectations of a lessened demand.

STATISTICS

PEAK (in months)	
Mean	Standard Deviation
-1.4	6.1

SERIES SCORES

Tables 9-1 and 9-2 provide the scores for many of the previous indicators.

Table 9-1: Series Scores: Inventories and Inventory Investment

Series	Timing			Conformity	Smoothness	Currency	Statistical Adequacy	Economic Significance	Revisions	Total		
	Peaks	Troughs	All Turns							Peaks	Troughs	All Turns
	(1)	(2)	(3)	(4)	(5)	(6)	(7)	(8)	(9)	(10)	(11)	(12)
Inventory Investment:												
30. Change in Business Inventories in 1972 Dollars	58	89	73	69	40	20	87	80	60	62	70	66
*36. Change in Mfg. and Trade Inventories on Hand and on Order in 1972 Dollars (Smoothed)	77	73	84	69	100	54	67	80	40	71	70	73
31. Change in Mfg. and Trade Inventoried, Book Value	33	39	59	69	0	54	72	80	80	55	56	61
38. Change in Manufacturers' Inventories, Materials and Supplies on Hand and on Order, Book Value	16	77	76	23	40	54	85	70	80	48	63	63

* A component of a major index.

Table 9-2: Series Scores: Inventories and Inventory Investment - Continued

Series	Timing				Smoothness	Currency	Statistical Adequacy	Economic Significance	Revisions	Total		
	Peaks	Troughs	All Turns	Conformity						Peaks	Troughs	All Turns
	(1)	(2)	(3)	(4)	(5)	(6)	(7)	(8)	(9)	(10)	(11)	(12)
Inventories on Hand and on Order;												
71. Mfg. and Trade Inventories, Book Value	90	82	96	71	100	54	72	80	60	77	75	79
70. Mfg. and Trade Inventories in 1972 Dollars	87	88	92	83	100	54	67	80	40	76	76	77
65. Manufacturers' Inventories, Finished Goods, Book Value	53	13	49	62	100	54	87	70	80	70	60	68
*77. Ratio, Mfg. and Trade Inventories to Sales in 1972 Dollars	93	80	80	66	60	54	70	80	60	73	70	70
78. Manufacturers' Inventories, Materials and Supplies on Hand and on Order, Book Value	9	76	81	68	100	54	85	70	80	59	76	77

* A component of a major index.

CHAPTER 10

PRICES, COSTS, AND PROFITS

The indicators utilized in this process are varied and include stock prices, commodity prices, profit margins, and cash flows. All of these indicators are shown in the table below.

As business cycle expansion takes place, profits generally increase. As expansion continues, competition for equipment, materials, and labor results in price increases. This can cause a peaking of a business cycle. Expectancies of business organizations' performance are reflected in stock prices.

Note that certain series include adjustments for IVA and CCAdj. These items are defined as follows:

- IVA, or Inventory Valuation Adjustment, is the change in the business-inventories component of Gross National Product (GNP). It is measured as the change in the physical volume of inventories valued in prices of the current period, less the change in the value of inventories reported by businesses (book value).

- CCAdj, or Capital Consumption Adjustment, is based upon an analysis of the capital consumption allowances, which are depreciation charges and accidental damages, to fixed business capital. For corporations, the CCAdj is the tax-return-based capital consumption allowances less capital consumption allowances that are based on estimates of uniform service lives, straight-line depreciation, and replacement costs.

SERIES	CATEGORY
Stock Prices, 500 Common Stocks	Stock Prices
Change in Producer Prices, Sensitive Materials	Sensitive Commodity Prices
Spot Market Prices, Raw Industrial Materials	Sensitive Commodity Prices
Change in Sensitive Material Prices (smoothed)	Profits and Profit Margins
Corporate Profits After Taxes	Profits and Profit Margins
Corporate Profits After Taxes in 1987 Dollars	Profits and Profit Margins
Corporate Profits After Tax with IVA and CCAdj*	Profits and Profit Margins
Corporate Profits After Tax with IVA and CCAdj in 1982 Dollars*	Profits and Profit Margins
Profits After Taxes per Dollar Sales, Mfg.*	Profits and Profit Margins
Ratio, Price to Unit Labor Cost, Nonfarm Business	Profits and Profit Margins
Ratio, Profits After Tax to Corporate Domestic Income	Profits and Profit Margins
Ratio, Profits After Tax With Adj. to Corporate Domestic Income	Profits and Profit Margins
Corporate Net Cash Flow	Cash Flows
Corporate Net Cash Flow in 1987 Dollars	Cash Flows

* Not reproduced by BEA.

STOCK PRICES

DESCRIPTION/DEFINITION

Index of Stock Prices (19) (M, Standard & Poor's Corporation) (L,L,L)
is an index of 500 stocks that measures the average price of stocks listed
on the New York Stock Exchange, American Stock Exchange, and the
NASDAQ National Market System, with 1941-43=100. The index includes 384 industrials, 45 utilities, 15 transportation, and 56 financial.
Each stock in the index is adjusted for rights, stock dividends, split-ups,
and mergers.

Exhibit 10-1

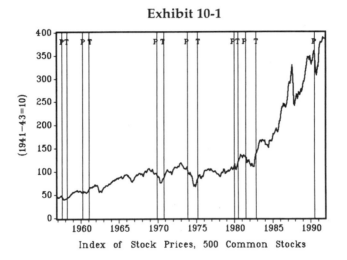

Index of Stock Prices, 500 Common Stocks

"Standard & Poor's 500" is a trademark of Standard & Poor's Corporation and this series is reproduced with permission of Standard and
Poor's.

SIGNIFICANCE

This index is a leading indicator of both peaks and troughs. Activity in
securities prices seems to reflect expectations. The level of securities markets influences financing undertaken by corporations and individuals for
equity funds. There are many other indexes which provide information

as to securities prices, i.e., the Dow Jones averages, Wilshire Index, Value Line Index, etc.

STATISTICS

PEAK (in months)		TROUGH (in months)	
Mean	Standard Deviation	Mean	Standard Deviation
-9.2	2.9	-2.8	2.8

SENSITIVE COMMODITY PRICES

DESCRIPTION/DEFINITION

Three series which reflect changes in materials prices and are expressed as percentage changes or as a constant 1967 =100 base are discussed.

Index of Producer Prices for Sensitive Crude and Intermediate Materials (98) (M,1 and 3) (L,L,L) is expressed as an index. It measures the month-to-month percent change in a producer price index for 28 intermediate and crude materials. The components include prices for the following commodities: cattle hides, natural rubber, six wastepaper components, seven iron and steel scrap components, three nonferrous metal components, five fiber components, four lumber and wood components, and sand, gravel, and crushed stone. Prices are seasonally adjusted prior to being combined into the 28-commodity index.

Exhibit 10-2

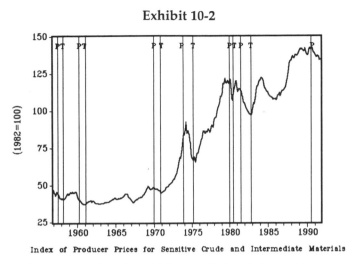

Index of Producer Prices for Sensitive Crude and Intermediate Materials

Change in Sensitive Materials Prices (99) (M, 1,3, and Commodity Research Bureau, Inc.) (L,L,L) is a smoothed, seasonally adjusted series using series 98, series 23, and the producer price index. It measures a change in the composite index derived through combining and adjusting the series.

Exhibit 10-3

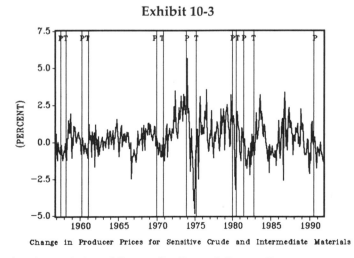

Change in Producer Prices for Sensitive Crude and Intermediate Materials

Reproduced with permission of Commodity Research Bureau, Inc.

Spot Market Prices, Raw Materials Industrial Materials (23) (M,3 and Commodity Research Bureau Inc.) (U,L,L) is an index with a 1967 = 100 base. It measures spot market price movement of a group of 13 raw industrial materials on commodity markets and organized exchanges. The commodities represent those presumed to be among the first to be influenced by changes in economic conditions. Spot is the price at which a commodity is selling for immediate delivery. Data is not seasonally adjusted.

Exhibit 10-4

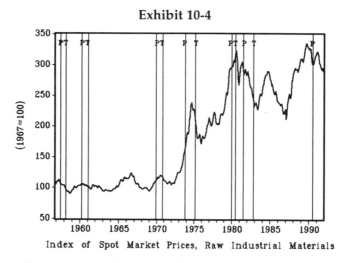

Index of Spot Market Prices, Raw Industrial Materials

Reproduced with permission of Commodity Research Bureau, Inc.

SIGNIFICANCE

Supply-and-demand relationships affect material prices. If the materials are starting to decline, one could have an indication of greater supply, indicating lessening use and, hence, peaking.

STATISTICS

SERIES	PEAK (in months)		TROUGH (in months)	
	Mean	Standard Deviation	Mean	Standard Deviation
Change in Producer Prices	-13.1	11.1	-9.1	6.2
Change in Sensitive Material Prices	-11.8	6.6	-2.8	2.8
Spot Market Prices	NA	NA	-0.3	4.6

PROFIT AND PROFIT MARGINS

DESCRIPTION/DEFINITION

The following discusses seven different series. These seven different series are composed of two rates, one profit per dollar of sale, and four series with major differences arising from their conversion from current to 1987 dollars. These series include inventory valuation adjustment (IVA), capital consumption allowances (CCA), and capital consumption adjustment (CCAdj).

Corporate Profits After Tax in Current Dollars (16) (Q,1) (L,L,L) is a quarterly indicator that measures corporate profits after tax and before IVA and CCAdj.

Exhibit 10-5

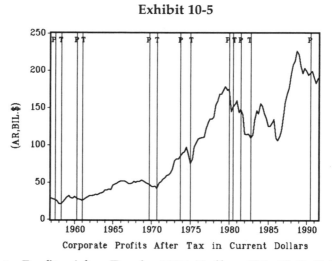

Corporate Profits After Tax in Current Dollars

Corporate Profits After Tax in 1987 Dollars (18) (Q,1) (L,L,L) is the
quarterly series above, deflated by breaking up the current dollars into
dividend and industrial profits components. The implicit price deflator
for personal consumption expenditures is used for dividends, and the
nonresidential fixed investment implicit price deflator is applied to undistributed profits.

Exhibit 10-6

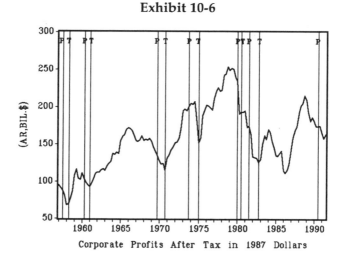

Corporate Profits After Tax in 1987 Dollars

Corporate Profits After Tax With IVA and CCAdj in Current Dollars (79) (Q,1) (L,C,L) is a quarterly series calculated in the same manner as series 16 above, adjusted for IVA and CCAdj.

Exhibit 10-7

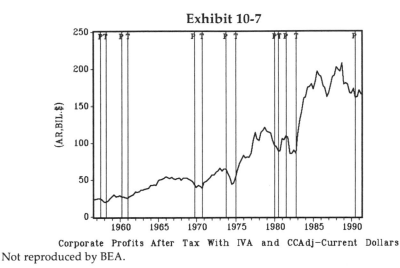

Corporate Profits After Tax With IVA and CCAdj–Current Dollars

Not reproduced by BEA.

Corporate Profits After Tax With IVA and CCAdj in 1982 Dollars (80) (Q,1) (L,C,L) is a quarterly series calculated in the same manner as series 18, with the adjustments for IVA and CCAdj.

Exhibit 10-8

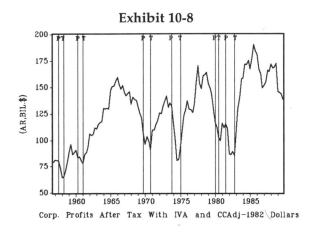

Corp. Profits After Tax With IVA and CCAdj–1982 Dollars

Not reproduced by BEA.

Ratio, Price to Unit Labor Cost (26) (Q,1) (L,L,L)   is a quarterly measure that is derived by dividing the implicit price deflator for GDP by
unit labor cost. Unit labor cost measures the labor compensation cost
required to produce one unit of output.

Exhibit 10-9

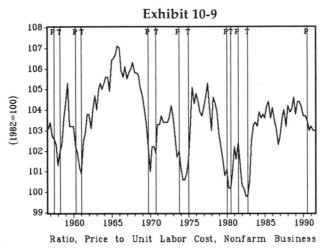

Ratio, Price to Unit Labor Cost, Nonfarm Business

**Ratio, Corporate Domestic Profits After Tax to Corporate Domestic In-
come (22) (Q,1) (L,L,L)**   is a quarterly measure of profits after tax origi-
nating in corporate domestic business as a percent of corporate domestic
income.

Exhibit 10-10

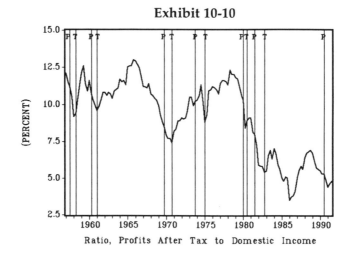

Ratio, Profits After Tax to Domestic Income

Ratio, Corporate Domestic Profits After Tax with IVA and CCAdj to Corporate Domestic Income (81) (Q,1) (U,L,L) is a quarterly measure related and constructed in the same manner as series 22 above, except that this series contains the IVA and CCAdj.

Exhibit 10-11

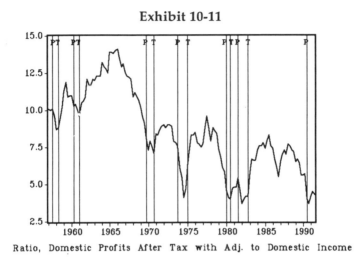

Ratio, Domestic Profits After Tax with Adj. to Domestic Income

Profits After Taxes Per Dollar of Sales, Manufacturing Corporations (15) (Q,2 and Federal Trade Commission; seasonal adjustment by Bureau of Economic Analysis) (L,L,L) is a quarterly indicator that includes a present sample of approximately 7,300 corporations drawn from a population of 280,000 corporations. All manufacturing corporations with assets greater than $25 million are included, as this category accounts for 87% of the total assets of manufacturing corporations. The data is seasonally adjusted.

Exhibit 10-12

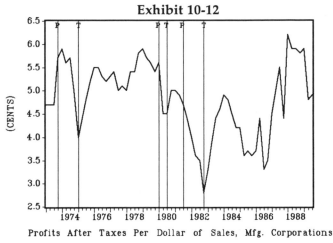

Profits After Taxes Per Dollar of Sales, Mfg. Corporations

Not supported or reproduced by BEA.

SIGNIFICANCE

A considerable lag between the events and reporting takes place, since the series are quarterly.

STATISTICS

SERIES	PEAK (in months)		TROUGH (in months)	
	Mean	Standard Deviation	Mean	Standard Deviation
Corporate Profits After Tax - Current	-7.0	8.7	-2.3	2.2
Corporate Profits After Tax - 1982	-10.4	10.4	-2.3	2.2
Corporate Profits After Tax With IVA and CCAdj Current	-14.7	14.8	0.7	7.1
Corporate After Tax With IVA and CCAdj 1982	-18.6	13.9	0.7	7.1
Ratio Corporate Profits/Income	-13.9	16.7	-2.3	2.2
Ratio Corporate Profits/Income IVA and CCAdj	NA	NA	0.3	7.0
Profits After Taxes Per Dollar Sales	-10.0	8.1	-2.3	2.2

CASH FLOW

DESCRIPTION/DEFINITION

Two series on corporate net cash flows are discussed. Generally, cash flows differ from reported net income due to large noncash deductions such as depreciation and amortization, which represents a cash flow.

Corporate Net Cash Flow in Current Dollars (34) (Q,1) (L,L,L) is   a quarterly reporting of the sum of undistributed corporate profits (the portion of profits remaining after taxes and dividends have been paid) and corporate capital consumption allowances.

Exhibit 10-13

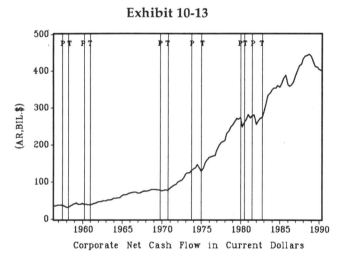

Corporate Net Cash Flow in Current Dollars

Not reproduced by BEA.

Corporate Net Cash Flow in 1987 Dollars (35) (Q,1) (L,L,L) is a quarterly reporting of the previous indicator in constant 1982 dollars.

Exhibit 10-14

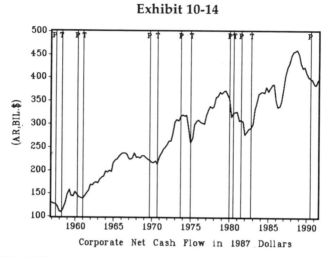

Corporate Net Cash Flow in 1987 Dollars

SIGNIFICANCE

Corporate net cash flow is required more than corporate profits after taxes because it reflects the long-term nature of amortization and depreciation changes.

STATISTICS

Both of these indicators are leading at both peaks and troughs.

SERIES	PEAK (in months)		TROUGH (in months)	
	Mean	Standard Deviation	Mean	Standard Deviation
Corporate Net Cash Flow in Current Dollars	-4.0	6.4	-3.6	3.0
Corporate Net Cash Flow in 1982 Dollars	-9.1	10.5	-2.3	2.2

SERIES SCORES

Tables 10-1 through 10-3 supply us with scores as to how well the indicators performed during expansion and contraction phases.

Table 10-1: Series Scores: Prices, Costs, and Profits

Series	Timing			Conformity	Smoothness	Currency	Statistical Adequacy	Economic Significance	Revisions	Total		
	Peaks	Troughs	All Turns							Peaks	Troughs	All Turns
	(1)	(2)	(3)	(4)	(5)	(6)	(7)	(8)	(9)	(10)	(11)	(12)
Sensitive Commodity Prices:												
98. Change in Producer Prices For 28 Sensitive Crude and Intermediate Materials	67	80	80	60	0	80	67	70	20	56	60	60
23. Index of Spot Market Prices, Raw Industrial Materials	0	56	28	71	100	100	77	70	100	63	77	70
*99. Change in Sensitive Materials Prices (Smoothed)	34	74	73	69	60	80	72	70	20	56	66	66
Stock Price:												
*19. Index of Stock Prices, 500 Common Stocks	41	92	94	65	80	100	80	80	100	72	85	85

* A component of a major index.

Table 10-2: Series Scores: Prices, Costs, and Profits - Continued (1)

| Series | Timing | | | Conformity | Smoothness | Currency | Statistical Adequacy | Economic Significance | Revisions | Total | | |
| | Peaks | Troughs | All Turns | | | | | | | Peaks | Troughs | All Turns |
	(1)	(2)	(3)	(4)	(5)	(6)	(7)	(8)	(9)	(10)	(11)	(12)
Profits and Profit Margins:												
16. Corporate Profits After Tax in Current Dollars	2	89	72	77	80	20	80	80	80	54	76	72
18. Corporate Profits AFter Tax in 1972 Dollars	27	89	77	76	60	20	80	80	80	58	74	71
79. Corporate Profits AFter Tax With IVA and CCAdj in Current Dollars	54	34	64	38	60	20	80	80	80	59	54	62
80. Corporate Profits After Tax With IVA and CCAdj in 1972 Dollars	54	34	64	45	60	20	80	80	80	60	55	63
22. Ratio, Profits After Tax to Total Corporate Domestic Income	27	89	77	80	60	20	80	80	80	59	74	71
81. Ratio, Profits After Tax With IVA and CCAdj to Total Corporate Domestic Income	27	34	53	37	60	20	80	80	80	52	54	59
15. Profits After Taxes Per Dollar of Sales, Mfg. Corporations	31	89	78	58	60	20	62	70	100	54	69	66
26. Ratio, Implicit Price Deflater to Unit Labor Cost, Nonfarm Business Sector	54	88	80	46	60	20	47	70	80	54	62	60

* A component of a major index.

Table 10-3: Series Scores: Prices, Costs, and Profits - Continued (2)

Series	Timing			Conformity	Smoothness	Currency	Statistical Adequacy	Economic Significance	Revisions	Total		
	Peaks	Troughs	All Turns							Peaks	Troughs	All Turns
	(1)	(2)	(3)	(4)	(5)	(6)	(7)	(8)	(9)	(10)	(11)	(12)
Cash Flows:												
34. Corporate Net Cash Flow in Current Dollars	7	88	85	80	80	20	80	70	80	54	74	74
35. Corporate Net Cash Flow in 1972 Dollars	27	89	77	79	60	20	80	70	80	57	73	70
Unit Labor Costs and Labor Share:												
63. Index of Unit Labor Cost, Business Sector	88	78	94	62	80	20	67	70	80	70	68	72
68. Labor Cost Per Unit of Real Gross Domestic Product, Nonfinancial Corporations	92	74	97	56	80	20	67	80	80	71	67	72
62. Index of Labor Cost Per Unit of Output, Mfg. — Actual Data	88	76	93	63	100	80	67	70	40	74	71	75
*62. Index of Labor Cost Per Unit of Output, Mfg. — Actual Data As a Percent of Trend	90	82	85	43	80	80	67	70	40	69	67	68
64. Compensation of Employees as a Percent of National Income	92	80	80	67	60	20	67	80	80	71	68	68

* A component of a major index.

CHAPTER 11

MONEY AND CREDIT

Money and credit provide the fuel for any business expansion. If credit is not available, expansion is difficult if not impossible. Generally, credit is based upon character, collateral, and capability. An examination of the series in this chapter provides several indicators that are addressed to the capability factor. Credit given freely and without regard to capability of repayment can and does result in delinquent loans and business failures. If widespread, this affects not only the borrower but also the lending institutions. This relationship is very apparent during the 1990s, when savings and loans and banks are going into bankruptcy in record numbers.

The price of money or interest is critical to decisions to invest in new plant and equipment, housing, or a new car. As those interest rates increase, expansion or purchase decisions are postponed to a later, more interest-favorable date. One notices that when interest rates start to decline, debt financing for long-term asset acquisition increases. What was not feasible at 12% becomes very attractive at 9%. The price of money can change rapidly if government intervention is present. This is easily apparent in the activities of the Federal Reserve Board in 1991, when the federal funds and the prime rate were decreased many times in an effort to stimulate the economy.

Many money and credit indicators are shown on the following series list.

SERIES	CATEGORY
Change in Money Supply M1	Money
Change in Money Supply M2	Money
Change in Total Liquid Assets*	Money
Money Supply M1 in 1982 Dollars	Money
Money Supply M2 in 1982 Dollars	Money
Net Change in Mortgage Debt*	Credit Flows
Net Change in Business Loans	Credit Flows
Net Change in Consumer Installment Credit	Credit Flows
Change in Business and Consumer Debt Outstanding	Credit Flows
Funds Raised by Private Nonfinancial Borrowers	Credit Flows
Delinquent Rate, Installment Loans	Credit Difficulties
Current Liabilities of Business Failures	Credit Difficulties
Free Reserves (Inverted)	Bank Reserves
Borrowing from the Federal Reserve	Bank Reserves
Federal Funds Rate	Interest Rates

* No longer reproduced by BEA.

MONEY

DESCRIPTION/DEFINITION

Five series dealing with money supply in constant dollars and changes in money supply, expressed as a percent, are discussed. The different money supply measures are popularly known as M1 and M2. In developing the indicators, deposits held by foreign banks, official government institutions, and the U.S. Government are excluded to avoid double counting. The major adjustment involves the netting of deposits held in depository institutions.

The M1 version of the money supply consists of

- Currency outside the Treasury, the Federal Reserve banks, and vaults of commercial banks.

- Outstanding amounts of U.S.-dollar-denominated travelers checks of nonbank issuers.

- Demand deposits of commercial banks and certain foreign-related institutions, less cash items in the process of collection, Federal Reserve float, and foreign demand balances at Federal Reserve banks.

- Interest-earning checkable deposits consisting of negotiable order of withdrawal (NOW) and automatic transfer accounts (ATS) at depository institutions other than credit unions, credit union share draft accounts and demand deposits at thrift institutions.

The M2 version of the money supply includes M1 plus

- Money market deposit accounts, savings, and small denomination time deposits (less than $100,000).

- Overnight and continuing repurchase agreements issued by commercial bands and certain overnight Eurodollars held by U.S. nonbank residents.

- Balances in both taxable and tax-exempt general purpose and broker/dealer money market mutual funds.

Keough and IRA balances at depository institutions and in money market mutual funds are excluded.

Estimates of M1 are available on a monthly and weekly basis, while estimates of M2 are only available monthly.

Total Liquid Assets include M2 plus

■ Large-denomination time deposits (over $100,000) at all depository institutions (including negotiable certificates of deposit), term repurchase agreements, and institution-only money market mutual fund shares.

■ Other liquid assets including nonbank public holdings of U.S. savings bonds, short-term treasury obligations, banker acceptances, commercial paper, and term Eurodollars held by U.S. residents.

Change in Money Supply M1 (85) (M,4) (L,L,L) is derived by computing month-to-month percent changes in the seasonally adjusted data for M1.

Exhibit 11-1

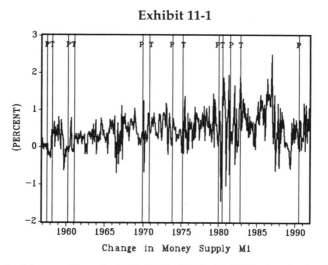

Change in Money Supply M1

Change in Money Supply M2 (102) (M,4) (L,C,U) is derived by computing the month-to-month percent changes in the seasonally adjusted data for M2.

Exhibit 11-2

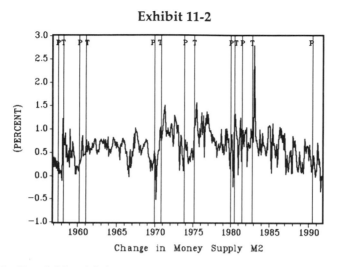

Change in Money Supply M2

Change in Total Liquid Assets (104) (M,1 and 4) (L,L,L)   is the result of
the smoothed moving average using the month-to-month percent
changes in total liquid assets.

This indicator will no longer be reproduced by the BEA. Current statistics are available through the Business Statistics branch, Bureau of
Economic Analysis.

Exhibit 11-3

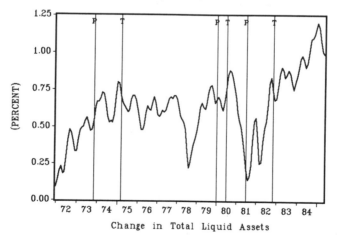

Change in Total Liquid Assets

No longer reproduced by BEA.

Money Supply M1 in 1982 Dollars (105) (M,1 and 4) (L,L,L) is a measure in constant dollars of M1 in current dollars deflated by the Consumer Price Index.

Exhibit 11-4

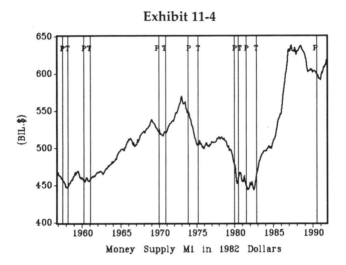

Money Supply M1 in 1982 Dollars

Money Supply M2 in 1982 Dollars (106) (M,1 and 4) (L,L,L) is a measure in constant dollars of M2 in current dollars deflated by the Consumer Price Index.

Exhibit 11-5

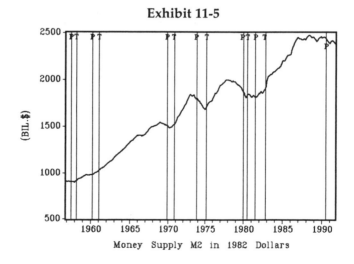

Money Supply M2 in 1982 Dollars

SIGNIFICANCE

As the money supply decreases, interest rates would be higher and money, of course, would be tighter, making prolonged expansion difficult. It would be interesting to find out what Fed chairman was in office at what time to see whether different policies and politics influenced M1 and M2.

STATISTICS

SERIES	PEAK (in months)		TROUGH (in months)	
	Mean	Standard Deviation	Mean	Standard Deviation
Change in Money Supply M1	-16.4	6.9	-8.1	7.8
Change in Money Supply M2	26.1	13.8	NA	NA
Change in Total Liquid Assets	-7.3	3.9	-7.7	5.0
Money Supply, M1 in 1982 Dollars	-13.3	7.3	-3.9	6.6
Money Supply, M2 in 1982 Dollars	-16.2	5.6	-5.6	4.6

CREDIT FLOWS

DESCRIPTION/DEFINITION

Five series, with all series being leading indicators of both peaks and troughs, are discussed.

Net Change in Mortgage Debt (33) (M,1,4, American Council of Life Insurance; Federal National Mortgage Association, U.S. Department of Housing and Urban Development, Government National Mortgage Association, National Association of Mutual Savings Banks, and Federal Home Loan Bank Board, seasonal adjustment by Bureau of Economic Analysis) (L,L,L) measures the month-to-month change in mortgage debt held by selected financial institutions and life insurance companies.

Exhibit 11-6

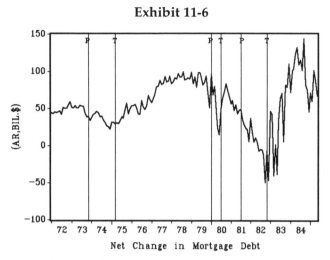

Net Change in Mortgage Debt

No longer supported or reproduced by BEA.

Net Change in Business Loans (112) (M,1,4, and The Federal Reserve Bank of New York) (L,L,L) measures the month-to-month amount of change in commercial and industrial loans outstanding.

Exhibit 11-7

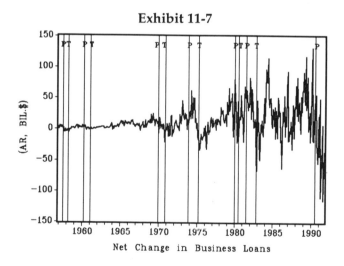

Net Change in Business Loans

Net Change in Consumer Installment Credit (113) (M,4) (L,L,L) measures the change during the month in the amount of consumer installment credit outstanding. It is defined as the amount of consumer installment credit extended, less the amount liquidated during the month.

Exhibit 11-8

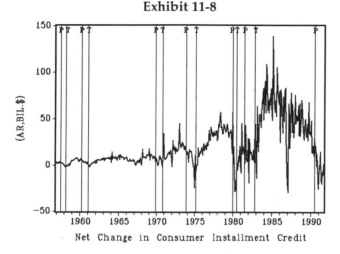

Net Change in Consumer Installment Credit

Change in Business and Consumer Credit Outstanding (111) (M,1,4, Federal Home Loan Bank Board, and the Federal Reserve Bank of New York) (L,L,L) is a result of combining series dealing with Consumer Installment Credit, Consumer and Industrial Loans, Mortgage Loans held by savings and loan associations, and Real Estate Loans of Weekly Reporting Large Commercial Banks. After combining the various series, the percent change is calculated.

Exhibit 11-9

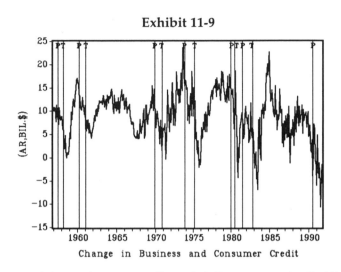

Change in Business and Consumer Credit

Funds Raised by Private Nonfinancial Borrowers (110) (Q,4) (L,L,L) measures the amount of funds raised less debt repaid each quarter in the U.S. credit markets by households, state and local governments, and nonfinancial businesses. Both domestic and foreign borrowers are included. The forms of credit covered are security issues, mortgages, consumer credit, business and farm loans from banks, federal loans to businesses and farms, commercial paper, and all security credit and loans to financial businesses are excluded.

Exhibit 11-10

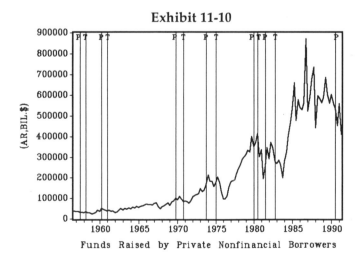

Funds Raised by Private Nonfinancial Borrowers

SIGNIFICANCE

Credit is necessary for business expansion and is not unlimited. Velocity changes of credit increases could be due to business contraction and/or a lack of funds with which to make loans. It may be interesting to see if there are any correlations between residential construction, sales, free reserves, etc., and possibly to come up with some indication of an overheated economy.

STATISTICS

SERIES	PEAK (in months)		TROUGH (in months)	
	Mean	Standard Deviation	Mean	Standard Deviation
Net Change in Mortgage Debt	-15.6	8.2	-3.4	3.9
Net Change in Business Loans	-10.7	9.0	-1.3	2.8
Net Change in Consumer Installment Credit	-11.4	7.5	-2.1	4.2
Change in Business and Consumer Credit Outstanding	12.7	5.5	-1.6	2.1
Funds Raised by Private Nonfinancial Borrower	11.2	5.2	-3.3	1.7

CREDIT DIFFICULTIES

DESCRIPTION/DEFINITION

Two series dealing with business failures and delinquent consumer installment loans are discussed below.

Current Liabilities of Business Failures (14) (M, Dun & Bradstreet, Inc.) defines a business failure as a concern that is involved in a court proceeding that is likely to end in a loss to creditors. Private households are excluded as well as major industries in the service sector.

Exhibit 11-11

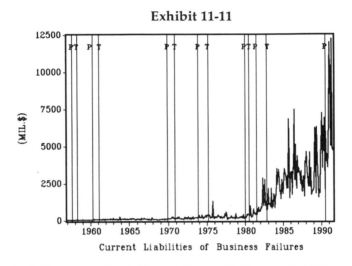

Current Liabilities of Business Failures

**Percent of Consumer Installment Loans Delinquent 30 Days and Over
(39) (EOM, American Bankers Association) (L,L,L)** measures installment loans having an installment past due for 30 days or more, using
data from 1800 commercial banks categorized by bank size in the 50
states and the District of Columbia.

Exhibit 11-12

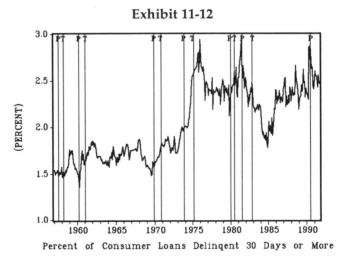

Percent of Consumer Loans Delinqent 30 Days or More

Both series are inversely related to broad movement in economic activities.

SIGNIFICANCE

Credit difficulty as shown by these series measures the extent of tight-ness of business credit. When money and credit are plentiful, one should see less failure and delinquency. An increase in delinquencies and fail-ures should indicate a slowdown in economic activities.

STATISTICS

Both these indicators are leading at both peaks and troughs.

SERIES	PEAK (in months)		TROUGH (in months)	
	Mean	Standard Deviation	Mean	Standard Deviation
Current Liabilities	-18.9	6.9	-8.1	7.8
Percent Delinquent	-8.7	7.1	-0.4	1.8

Source: Board of Governors of the Federal Reserve System

BANK RESERVES

DESCRIPTION/ DEFINITION

There are two series used for bank reserves, and both the series are clas-sified as leading indicators at peaks of business cycles. The indicators are:

THE SERIES AND THE SIGNIFICANCE

Free Reserves (93) (M,4) (L,U,U). This series measures the difference be-tween the excess reserves of member banks and their borrowing from the Federal Reserves System. When excess reserves exceed total borrow-ing, the difference is termed "free reserves." When borrowings exceed excess reserves, the difference is termed "net borrowed reserves." The amount of free reserves is a partial reflection of the bank system's ability to make more loans. As free reserves increase, interest rates are generally lower than in a period when net borrowed reserves are high.

Exhibit 11-13

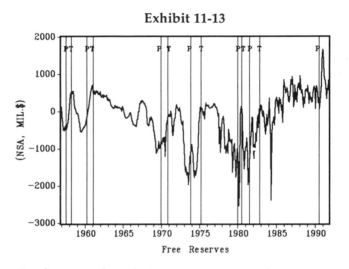

Free Reserves

Member Bank Borrowings (94) (M,4) (L,Lg,U). This is the amount member banks have borrowed on a temporary basis to meet reserve requirements.

Exhibit 11-14

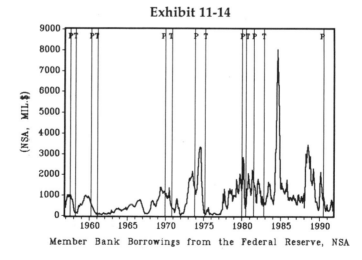

Member Bank Borrowings from the Federal Reserve, NSA

STATISTICS

SERIES	PEAK (in months)	
	Mean	Standard Deviation
Free Reserves	-2.5	6.4
Member Bank Borrowing	-1.7	6.0

THE FEDERAL FUNDS RATE

DESCRIPTION/DEFINITION

Federal Funds Rate (119) (M,4) (C,Lg,Lg). Federal funds are those funds which represent excess reserves to one bank and are transferred to other banks that have a shortage of reserves. These funds are made available by a number of institutions, and the usage charge of these funds is referred to as the federal funds rate. The rate is usually for over-night use.

Exhibit 11-15

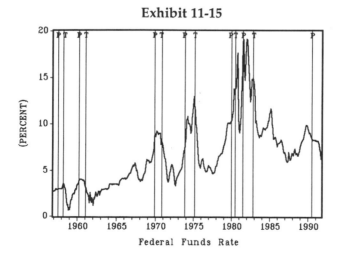

Federal Funds Rate

SIGNIFICANCE

This is a highly responsive short-term, tight-money indicator. The rate is normally at or above the T-Bill rate (adjusted to annual rate) and represents an employment of capital for short-term purposes. There are many other indicators for interest rates which differ in their measurement as to the term of the security and quality.

STATISTICS

PEAKS (in months)	
Mean	Standard Deviation
0.8	4.8

SERIES SCORES

Tables 11-1 through 11-5 reflect the scores of these indicators at peaks and troughs.

Table 11-1: Series Scores: Money and Credit

| Series | Timing | | | Conformity | Smoothness | Currency | Statistical Adequacy | Economic Significance | Revisions | Total | | |
	Peaks	Troughs	All Turns							Peaks	Troughs	All Turns
	(1)	(2)	(3)	(4)	(5)	(6)	(7)	(8)	(9)	(10)	(11)	(12)
Money:												
85. Change in Money Supply M1	74	80	80	52	0	100	100	80	80	71	73	73
102. Change in Money Supply M2	67	80	80	52	0	80	85	80	80	65	69	69
104. Change in Total Liquid Assets (Smoothed)	39	78	89	61	100	27	100	80	20	61	70	73
105. Money Supply M1 in 1972 Dollars	72	77	80	58	100	80	100	80	80	80	81	82
*106. Money Supply M2 in 1972 Dollars	9	67	54	29	100	80	85	80	80	58	72	69
Velocity of Money												
107. Ratio, Gross National Product to Money Supply M1	78	11	71	63	80	20	85	80	60	70	53	68
108. Ratio, Personal Income to Money Supply M2	71	65	77	71	80	80	81	80	60	75	73	76

* A component of a major composite index.

Table 11-2: Money and Credit - Continued (1)

Series	Timing			Conformity	Smoothness	Currency	Statistical Adequacy	Economic Significance	Revisions	Total		
	Peaks	Troughs	All Turns							Peaks	Troughs	All Turns
	(1)	(2)	(3)	(4)	(5)	(6)	(7)	(8)	(9)	(10)	(11)	(12)
Credit Flows:												
33. Net Changes in Mortgage Debt	57	85	80	90	40	54	72	70	40	62	69	68
112. Net Change in Business Loans	29	84	75	76	0	80	57	80	60	53	67	65
113. Net Change in Consumer Installment Credit	71	70	77	76	40	54	100	80	100	76	75	77
*111. Change in Business and Consumer Credit Outstanding	72	57	75	76	40	80	74	80	60	70	67	71
110. Funds Raised by Private Nonfinancial Borrowers in Credit Markets	71	94	88	91	40	20	98	80	80	72	78	76

* A component of a major composite index.

Table 11-3: Series Scores: Money and Credit - Continued (2)

Series	Timing			Conformity	Smoothness	Currency	Statistical Adequacy	Economic Significance	Revisions	Total		
	Peaks	Troughs	All Turns							Peaks	Troughs	All Turns
	(1)	(2)	(3)	(4)	(5)	(6)	(7)	(8)	(9)	(10)	(11)	(12)
Credit Difficulties:												
14. Current Liabilities of Business Failures (Inverted)	70	66	78	81	0	27	67	70	100	63	62	65
39. Percent of Consumer Installment Loans Delinquent 30 Days and Over (Inverted)	33	78	83	73	60	27	40	60	100	53	64	65
Bank Reserves:												
93. Free Reserves (Inverted)	63	53	71	26	60	100	85	70	80	67	64	69
94. Member Bank Borrowings From the Federal Reserve	8	65	67	73	60	100	85	70	80	60	74	75

Table 11-4: Series Scores: Money and Credit - Continued (3)

Series	Timing			Conformity	Smoothness	Currency	Statistical Adequacy	Economic Significance	Revisions	Total		
	Peaks	Troughs	All Turns							Peaks	Troughs	All Turns
	(1)	(2)	(3)	(4)	(5)	(6)	(7)	(8)	(9)	(10)	(11)	(12)
Interest Rates:												
119. Federal Funds Rate	81	75	79	82	100	100	80	80	100	87	85	86
114. Discount Rate on New Issues of 91-Day Treasury Bills	87	65	81	93	80	100	85	80	100	88	83	87
116. Yield on New Issues of High-grade Corporate Bonds	85	34	75	90	60	100	80	80	100	85	72	82
115. Yield on Long-Term Treasury Bonds	87	73	85	81	60	100	80	80	100	84	80	83
117. Yield on Municipal Bonds, 20-Bond Average	76	77	80	25	60	100	100	80	100	76	76	77
118. Secondary Market Yields on FHA Mortgages	92	77	80	80	100	80	59	80	100	84	80	81
67. Bank Rates on Short-Term Business Loans	92	80	86	80	60	20	57	80	100	74	71	72
*109. Average Prime Rate Charges by Banks	94	77	80	70	100	100	100	80	100	91	87	88

* A component of a major composite index.

Table 11-5: Series Scores: Money and Credit - Continued (4)

Series	Timing			Conformity	Smoothness	Currency	Statistical Adequacy	Economic Significance	Revisions	Total		
	Peaks	Troughs	All Turns							Peaks	Troughs	All Turns
	(1)	(2)	(3)	(4)	(5)	(6)	(7)	(8)	(9)	(10)	(11)	(12)
Outstanding Debt:												
66. Consumer Installment Credit Outstanding	29	11	20	59	100	54	100	80	100	69	64	66
72. Commercial and Industrial Loans Outstanding in Current Dollars	82	65	85	72	100	80	57	80	60	76	72	77
*101. Commercial and Industrial Loans Outstanding in 1972 Dollars	91	77	88	85	100	80	57	80	60	80	76	79
*95. Ratio, Consumer Installment Credit Outstanding to Personal Income	86	90	95	66	100	54	81	80	60	77	78	79

* A component of a major composite index.

PART III

COMPOSITE INDEXES
AND
OTHER MEASURES

CHAPTER 12

COMPOSITE INDEXES

Since the causes of a business cycle trend change can vary, so might the behavior of an individual indicator. Most of the included indicators have observed regularities, but one indicator alone may not provide anticipatory or predictive information as to a particular business cycle. This is the reason for the inclusion of indicators from different economic processes. This inclusion allows an observer to estimate the materiality of change to the whole economy instead of to an individual part of the economy. The degree of predicted change can be more certain if the change is shown to be diffused throughout the economy.

A COMPOSITE INDEX

Rather than depend upon one indicator, a composite index is constructed using indicators that have high scores in predicting or confirming peaks and troughs. These high scores are the result of using the scoring methods for indicators discussed in Chapter 1. Use of an index can result in a more dependable interpretation for the following reasons:

- Increases the chances of getting a correct signal, as the index represents many indicators from different economic processes.

- Reduces possible interpretation errors due to errors in underlying observations. If mistakes are independent, the use of many indicators instead of only one can prevent improper analysis.

- Month-to-month fluctuations of individual indicators can be quite erratic. Just as in an average, an index has a smoothing effect since its has many components, not one.

Inclusion in an Index

To be included in a composite index, reliable data must be available in a timely manner. This is a reason why most leading, lagging, and coincident indicators are of a monthly nature. Some often-quoted indicators suffer from being of a quarterly nature and are subject to a material amount of revision. Gross National Product (GNP) is an example of this, as previously discussed.

Index Construction, Revision and Development

The Bureau of Economic Research is constantly searching for better methods and measures to help predict peaks and troughs in the business cycle. Hertzberg and Beckman, in the January 1989 edition of the *Business Conditions Digest*, discuss this process and the possible needs for more representative indicators in the future. The importance of service-sector-related indicators and the work of Geoffrey H. Moore of the Center for International Business Cycle Research are cited.

Not only the BEA, but many other organizations are searching for better indicators, many of which may be components of future composite indexes. Many of the organizations previously identified as sources of information have their own copyrighted indexes and indicators developed as a result of independent research.

Revision of indexes may result in components being dropped and others added, as well as the adoption of improved statistical methods such as smoothing, or procedural changes relating to an adjustment of trend factors, or a different method of standardization as between the indicators included in any composite index.

THE COMPOSITE INDEX OF LEADING INDICATORS

Eleven of the leading indicators were chosen on the basis of their qualities and overall results over many cycles. The indicators included in this composite index follow.

By Economic Process, Series Number, and Indicators
I. Employment and Unemployment
(1) Average Weekly Hours, Mfg.
(5) Average Weekly Initial Claims (inverted)
II. Consumption, Trade Orders, and Delivery
(8) Manufacturers' New Orders in 1982 Dollars-Consumer Goods and Materials
(32) Vendor Performance
(83) Index of Consumer Expectation
(92) Change in Manufacturers' Unfilled Orders in 1982 Dollars, Durable Goods (smoothed)
III. Fixed Capital Investment
(20) Contracts and Orders for Plant and Equipment in 1982 Dollars
(29) Index of New Private Housing Units Authorized by Local Building Permits
IV. Prices, Costs, and Profits
(19) Index of Stock Prices, 500 Common Stocks
(99) Change in Sensitive Materials Prices (smoothed)
V. Money and Credit
(106) Money Supply M2 in 1982 Dollars

Table 12-1

Series No.	Series Title							

LEADING INDICATORS

Specific peak dates corresponding to reference peaks in —

Series No.	Series Title	July 1981	Jan. 1980	Nov. 1973	Dec. 1969	Apr. 1960	Aug. 1957	July 1953
1	Average weekly hours, mfg.	12/80 (-10)	3/79 (-10)	4/73 (-7)	10/68 (-14)	5/59 (-11)	11/55 (-21)	4/53 (-3)
5	Average weekly initial claims (inverted)	7/81 (0)	9/78 (-16)	2/73 (-9)	1/69 (-11)	4/59 (-12)	9/55 (-23)	9/52 (-10)
8	Mfrs.' new orders in 1982 dollars, consumer goods and materials	10/80 (-9)	12/78 (-13)	3/73 (-8)	11/68 (-13)	2/59 (-14)	7/55 (-25)	4/53 (-3)
32	Vendor performance, slower deliveries diffusion index	4/81 (-3)	4/79 (-9)	11/73 (0)	8/69 (-4)	2/59 (-14)	4/55 (-28)	7/52 (-12)
20	Contracts and orders for plant and equipment in 1982 dollars	4/81 (-3)	3/79 (-10)	10/72 (-1)	4/69 (-8)	3/59 (-13)	11/56 (-9)	2/53 (-5)
29	Building permits, new private housing units	9/80 (-10)	6/78 (-19)	12/72 (-11)	2/69 (-10)	11/58 (-17)	2/55 (-30)	11/52 (-8)
92	Chg. in mfrs.' unf. orders in 1982 dollars, durable goods (smoothed)	12/80 (-7)	12/78 (-13)	5/73 (-6)	5/69 (-7)	4/59 (-12)	1/56 (-19)	5/51 (-26)
99	Change in sensitive materials prices (smoothed¹)	12/80 (-7)	5/79 (-8)	1/74 (+2)	2/69 (-10)	11/58 (-17)	8/55 (-24)	6/53 (-1)
19	Index of stock prices, 500 common stocks	11/80 (-8)	NST	1/73 (-10)	12/68 (-12)	7/59 (-9)	7/56 (-13)	1/53 (-6)
106	Money supply M2 in 1982 dollars	NST	1/78 (-24)	1/73 (-10)	1/69 (-11)	NST	1/56 (-19)	NST
83	Index of consumer expectations	5/81 (-2)	11/76 (-38)	8/72 (-15)	2/69 (-10)	2/60 (-2)	11/56 (-9)	2/53 (-5)
910	Composite index of 11 leading indicators	5/81 (-2)	10/78 (-15)	3/73 (-8)	4/69 (-8)	6/59 (-10)	12/55 (-20)	2/53 (-5)
940	Ratio, coincident index to lagging index	10/80 (-9)	4/78 (-21)	12/72 (-11)	11/68 (-13)	4/59 (-12)	5/55 (-27)	10/52 (-9)

LEADING INDICATORS

Specific trough dates corresponding to reference troughs in —

Series No.	Series Title	Nov. 1982	July 1980	Mar. 1975	Nov. 1970	Feb. 1961	Apr. 1958	May 1954
1	Average weekly hours, mfg.	10/82 (-1)	7/80 (0)	3/75 (0)	9/70 (-2)	12/60 (-2)	4/58 (0)	4/54 (-1)
5	Average weekly initial claims (inverted)	9/82 (-2)	5/80 (-2)	3/75 (0)	10/70 (-1)	2/61 (0)	4/58 (0)	9/54 (+4)
8	Mfrs.' new orders in 1982 dollars, consumer goods and materials	10/82 (-1)	6/80 (-1)	3/75 (0)	11/70 (0)	1/61 (-1)	4/58 (0)	10/53 (-7)
32	Vendor performance, slower deliveries diffusion index	3/82 (-8)	5/80 (-2)	2/75 (-1)	12/70 (+1)	3/60 (-11)	12/57 (-4)	11/53 (-6)
20	Contracts and orders for plant and equipment in 1982 dollars	8/82 (-3)	5/80 (-2)	12/75 (+9)	10/70 (-1)	3/61 (+1)	3/58 (-1)	3/54 (-2)
29	Building permits, new private housing units	10/81 (-13)	4/80 (-3)	3/75 (0)	1/70 (-10)	12/60 (-2)	2/58 (-2)	9/53 (-8)
92	Chg. in mfrs.' unf. orders in 1982 dollars, durable goods (smoothed)	9/82 (-2)	6/80 (-1)	4/75 (+1)	8/70 (-3)	5/60 (-9)	2/58 (-2)	12/53 (-5)
99	Change in sensitive materials prices (smoothed¹)	4/82 (-7)	7/80 (0)	1/75 (-2)	9/70 (-2)	1/61 (-1)	1/58 (-3)	1/54 (-4)
19	Index of stock prices, 500 common stocks	7/82 (-4)	NST	12/74 (-3)	6/70 (-5)	10/60 (-4)	12/57 (-3)	9/53 (-8)
106	Money supply M2 in 1982 dollars	NST	5/80 (-2)	1/75 (-2)	4/70 (-7)	NST	1/58 (-3)	NST
83	Index of consumer expectations	3/82 (-8)	3/80 (-4)	2/75 (-1)	5/70 (-6)	11/60 (-3)	5/58 (+1)	11/53 (-6)
910	Composite index of 11 leading indicators	1/82 (-10)	5/80 (-2)	2/75 (-1)	10/70 (-1)	4/60 (-10)	2/58 (-2)	11/53 (-6)
940	Ratio, coincident index to lagging index	1/82 (-10)	5/80 (-2)	3/75 (0)	11/70 (0)	2/61 (0)	3/58 (-1)	12/53 (-5)

Table 12-1 shows the differences in results of the individual indicators making up the composite index of leading indicators and the composite index relative to the peak and trough dates established by the National Bureau of Economic Research. It also includes other leading indicators not included in the Composite Index.

If one were to calculate the mean and the standard deviation for each month using additional data since the 1984 study, one may find that these new means and standard deviations differ from those reported in the individual indicators statistics reported.

This index's behavior is shown graphically below.

Composite Index of 11 Leading Indicators (910) (M,1). Described above.

Exhibit 12-1

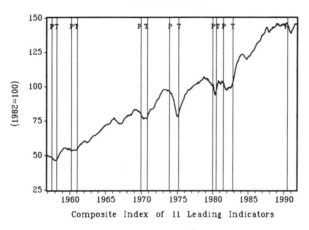

Composite Index of 11 Leading Indicators

STATISTICS

PEAK (in months)		TROUGHS (in months)	
Mean	Standard Deviation	Mean	Standard Deviation
-10.6	5.5	-2.0	-2.6

Note: In 1984, when these statistics were published, there were 12 leading indicators making up the composite indicators, namely, series 1, 5, 8, 12, 19, 20, 29, 32, 36, 99, 106, and 111. Since then, series 92 and 83 were added and series 12, 36, and 111 were deleted.

ALTERNATIVE LEADING INDEXES

The Center for International Business Cycle Research (CIBCR) at Columbia University has developed two composite indexes, which are shown monthly in the *Survey of Current Business*. These two indexes differ in the degree in which they are leading. These indexes also differ from those of the BEA's indicators used for their forecasting. Both of the indexes are reproduced with the permission of CIBCR, the copyright holder.

CIBCR Long-Leading Composite Index (990) (M,CIBCR)

Exhibit 12-2

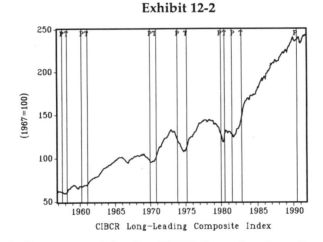

CIBCR Long-Leading Composite Index

The indicators used in the CIBCR Long-Leading Composite Index are:

Title / Source
Building Permits for New Private Housing Units   BCI(29)
Bond Prices   Dow Jones
Ratio of Price to Unit Labor Cost in Manufacturing   CIBCR
Deflated M2 Money Supply   BCI(106)

This index has only four components, as contrasted to the eleven leading indicators used by the BEA in their composite.

CIBCR Short-Leading Composite Index (991) (M,CIBCR)

Exhibit 12-3

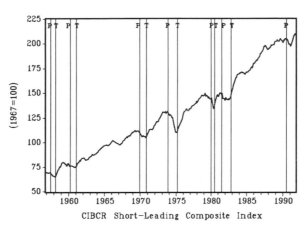

CIBCR Short-Leading Composite Index

The indicators used in the CIBCR Short-Leading Composite Index are:

Title / Source
Average Weekly Hours in Manufacturing   BCI(1)
Average Weekly Initial Claims for Unemployment Insurance   BCI(5)
Layoff Rate Under 5 Weeks   CIBCR
Deflated New Orders for Consumer Goods and Material   BCI(8)
Vendor Performance   BCI(32)
Change in Business Population   CIBCR
Deflated Contracts and Orders for Plant and Equipment   BCI(20)
Inventory Changes   National Association of Purchasing Management
Change in Industrial Material Prices   Journal of Commerce
Stock Prices   BCI(19)
Change in Deflated Total Debt   CIBCR

All indicators have not been recognized by the BEA as business cycle indicators. In the CIBCR composite indexes, two different BCI indicators, additional indicators developed by CIBCR, and other organizations' indicators are used.

Geoffrey Moore at Columbia University has been especially active in the study and development of indicators and measures. As editor of *Business Cycle Indicators* (1961), as a contributor to Gordon (1986) and Fabozzi and Greenfield (1984), his writings should be examined to provide background and methodology to any study of indicators.

COMPOSITE INDEX OF FOUR COINCIDENT INDICATORS

Coincident indicators tend to summarize the state of actual business activity. These indicators can confirm or invalidate expectations based upon the behavior of the leading indicators. Policy decisions, on a wait-and-see basis after signals from leading indicators, can now be implemented or discarded.

The indicators included in the Coincident Index are shown next.

By Economic Process, Series Number, and Indicators
I. Employment and Unemployment
(41) Employees on Nonagricultural Payrolls
II. Production and Income
(51) Personal Incomes Less Transfer Payments in 1982 Dollars
(47) Index of Industrial Production
III. Consumption, Trade Orders, and Deliveries
(57) Manufacturing and Trade Sales in 1982 Dollars

The comparison of actual indicator and index results with that of peaks and troughs is shown in Table 12-2.

Table 12-2

Specific peak dates corresponding to reference peaks in —

Series No.	Series Title	July 1953	Aug. 1957	Apr. 1960	Dec. 1969	Nov. 1973	Jan. 1980	July 1981
	COINCIDENT INDICATORS							
41	Employees on nonagricultural payrolls	6/53 (-1)	3/57 (-5)	4/60 (0)	3/70 (+3)	10/74 (+11)	3/80 (+2)	7/81 (0)
51	Personal income less transfer payments in 1982 dollars	10/53 (+3)	8/57 (0)	6/60 (+2)	NST	11/73 (0)	1/80 (0)	8/81 (+1)
47	Index of industrial production	7/53 (0)	3/57 (-5)	1/60 (-3)	10/69 (-2)	11/73 (0)	3/80 (+2)	7/81 (0)
57	Mfg. and trade sales in 1982 dollars	4/53 (-3)	2/57 (-6)	1/60 (-3)	10/69 (-2)	11/73 (0)	3/79 (-10)	1/81 (-6)
920	Composite index of 4 coincident indicators	7/53 (0)	2/57 (-6)	1/60 (-3)	10/69 (-2)	11/73 (0)	1/80 (0)	7/81 (0)

Specific trough dates corresponding to reference troughs in —

Series No.	Series Title	May 1954	Apr. 1958	Feb. 1961	Nov. 1970	Mar. 1975	July 1980	Nov. 1982
	COINCIDENT INDICATORS							
41	Employees on nonagricultural payrolls	8/54 (+3)	5/58 (+1)	2/61 (0)	11/70 (0)	4/75 (+1)	7/80 (0)	12/80 (+1)
51	Personal income less transfer payments in 1982 dollars	4/54 (-1)	4/58 (0)	12/60 (-2)	NST	2/75 (-1)	7/80 (0)	7/81 (-2)
47	Index of industrial production	4/54 (-1)	4/58 (0)	2/61 (0)	11/70 (0)	3/75 (0)	7/80 (0)	10/80 (+1)
57	Mfg. and trade sales in 1982 dollars	12/53 (-5)	4/58 (0)	1/61 (-1)	11/70 (0)	3/75 (0)	6/80 (-1)	4/81 (-1)
920	Composite index of 4 coincident indicators	8/54 (+3)	4/58 (0)	2/61 (0)	11/70 (0)	3/75 (0)	7/80 (0)	10/80 (+1)

Behavior of this index seems consistent with its being named coincident.

Composite Index of 4 Coincident Indicators (920) (M,1)

Exhibit 12-4

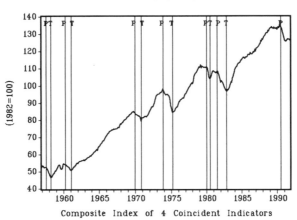

Composite Index of 4 Coincident Indicators

STATISTICS

PEAK (in months)		TROUGHS (in months)	
Mean	Standard Deviation	Mean	Standard Deviation
-2.0	1.9	0.4	1.0

Note: The series used in the composites are unchanged since the statistical study in 1984.

THE INDIVIDUAL INDICATORS

EMPLOYMENT AND UNEMPLOYMENT

Employees on Nonagricultural Payrolls (41) (M,3) (C,C,C) measures
the number of persons employed in nonagricultural establishments. The
industries include mining, utilities, wholesale and retail trade, finance,
insurance, and real estate, services, and government.

Exhibit 12-5

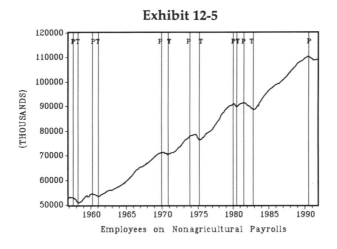

Employees on Nonagricultural Payrolls

PRODUCTION AND INCOME

**Personal Incomes Less Transfer Payments in 1982 Dollars (51) (M,1)
(C,C,C)** measures personal income less transfer payments (as described
by the title). Because transfer payments represent the largest part of personal income that does not accrue in production and because some types
of transfer payments tend to be contracyclical, their removal from personal income provides a series with greater cyclical amplitude.

Exhibit 12-6

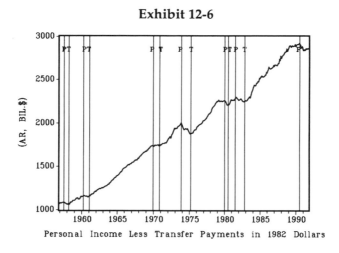

Personal Income Less Transfer Payments in 1982 Dollars

Index of Industrial Production (47) (M,4) (C,C,C) is computed by combining series covering all stages of production in manufacturing, mining, and gas and electric utility industries.

Exhibit 12-7

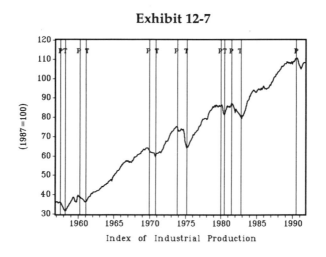

Index of Industrial Production

CONSUMPTION, TRADE ORDERS , AND DELIVERY

Manufacturing and Trade Sales in 1982 Dollars (57) (M,1 and 2) (C,C,C) measures the monthly sales volume of manufacturing, merchant wholesalers, and retail establishments in 1982 dollars. Appropriate components of the Producers Price Indexes are used to deflate manufacturing and wholesale, with the Consumer Price Indexes applied to retail sales. Applicable weights are applied to the makeup of sales within the categories.

Exhibit 12-8

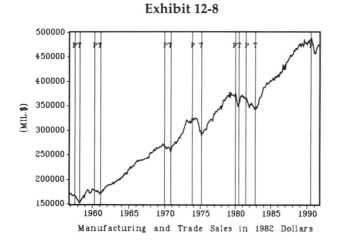

Manufacturing and Trade Sales in 1982 Dollars

THE COMPOSITE INDEX OF SEVEN LAGGING INDICATORS

The purpose of this index is to confirm or refute the inferences derived from the behavior of the coincident indicators. In forecasting, its value is in giving advance notice of a possible turn in leading indicators.

Composition of this index is shown next.

By Economic Process, Series Number, and Indicator
I. Employment and Unemployment
(91) Average Duration of Unemployment
II. Inventories and Inventory Investment
(77) Ratio, Manufacturing and Trade Inventories to Sales in 1982 Dollars
III. Prices, Costs, and Profits
(62) Change in Index of Labor Cost Per Unit of Output, Mfg. (smoothed)
(120) Change in Consumer Price Index for Services (smoothed)
IV. Money and Credit
(109) Average Prime Rate Charged by Banks
(101) Commercial and Industrial Loans Outstanding in 1982 Dollars
(95) Ratio, Consumer Installment Credit Outstanding to Personal Income

The results over many periods of using the individual and the composite indexes are shown in Table 12-3.

Table 12-3

LEADING INDICATORS — Specific peak dates corresponding to reference peaks in —

Series No.	Series Title	July 1953	Aug. 1957	Apr. 1960	Dec. 1969	Nov. 1973	Jan. 1980	July 1981
91	Average duration of unemployment (inverted)	9/53 (+2)	9/57 (+1)	6/60 (+2)	10/69 (-2)	9/73 (-2)	7/79 (-6)	12/81 (+5)
77	Ratio, mfg. and trade inventories to sales in 1982 dollars	12/53 (+5)	4/58 (+8)	1/61 (+11)	11/70 (+11)	3/75 (+16)	6/80 (+5)	10/82 (+15)
62	Change in index of labor cost per unit of output, mfg. (smoothed)	1/54 (+6)	3/58 (+7)	2/61 (+10)	1/70 (+1)	3/75 (+16)	6/80 (+5)	1/82 (+6)
109	Average prime rate charged by banks	2/54 (+7)	12/57 (+4)	7/60 (+3)	2/70 (+2)	9/74 (+10)	4/80 (+3)	8/81 (+1)
101	Commercial and industrial loans outstanding in 1982 dollars	6/53 (-1)	9/57 (+1)	NST	8/70 (+8)	9/74 (+10)	3/80 (+2)	9/82 (+14)
95	Ratio, consumer installment credit to personal income	4/54 (+9)	1/58 (+5)	12/60 (+8)	NST	4/74 (+5)	11/79 (-2)	NST
120	Change in Consumer Price Index for services (smoothed)	NA	3/57 (-5)	10/59 (-6)	4/70 (+4)	10/74 (+11)	6/80 (+5)	9/81 (+2)
930	Composite index of 7 lagging indicators	12/53 (+5)	12/57 (+4)	7/60 (+3)	3/70 (+3)	12/74 (+13)	4/80 (+3)	9/81 (+2)

LEADING INDICATORS — Specific trough dates corresponding to reference troughs in —

Series No.	Series Title	May 1954	Apr. 1958	Feb. 1961	Nov. 1970	Mar. 1975	July 1980	Nov. 1982
91	Average duration of unemployment (inverted)	5/55 (+12)	10/58 (+6)	7/61 (+5)	6/72 (+19)	1/76 (+10)	1/81 (+6)	7/83 (+8)
77	Ratio, mfg. and trade inventories to sales in 1982 dollars	4/55 (+11)	5/59 (+13)	4/62 (+14)	2/73 (+27)	11/78 (+44)	1/81 (+6)	1/84 (+14)
62	Change in index of labor cost per unit of output, mfg. (smoothed)	4/55 (+11)	11/58 (+7)	9/61 (+7)	11/71 (+12)	11/75 (+8)	7/81 (+12)	8/83 (+9)
109	Average prime rate charged by banks	7/55 (+14)	8/58 (+4)	11/65 (+57)	3/72 (+16)	4/77 (+25)	8/80 (+1)	7/83 (+8)
101	Commercial and industrial loans outstanding in 1982 dollars	8/54 (+3)	8/58 (+4)	NST	2/72 (+15)	9/76 (+18)	3/81 (+8)	10/83 (+11)
95	Ratio, consumer installment credit to personal income	11/54 (+6)	11/58 (+7)	11/61 (+9)	NST	2/76 (+11)	NST	11/82 (0)
120	Change in Consumer Price Index for services (smoothed)	NA	12/58 (+8)	7/61 (+5)	2/73 (+27)	8/75 (+5)	10/80 (+3)	1/83 (+2)
930	Composite index of 7 lagging indicators	2/55 (+9)	8/58 (+4)	8/61 (+6)	2/72 (+15)	6/76 (+15)	10/80 (+3)	6/83 (+7)

The behavior of this index is shown below.

Composite Index of 7 Lagging Indicators (930) (M,1)

Exhibit 12-9

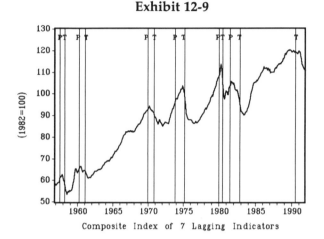

Composite Index of 7 Lagging Indicators

PEAK (in months)		TROUGHS (in months)	
Mean	Standard Deviation	Mean	Standard Deviation
5.1	3.4	10.0	3.3

Note: Since 1984, series 11 and 120 were added to the series making up this composite.

THE INDIVIDUAL INDICATORS

EMPLOYMENT AND UNEMPLOYMENT

Average Duration of Unemployment (91) (M,3) (Lg,Lg,Lg) measures the average number of weeks, including the current survey week, during which persons classified as unemployed had been continuously looking for work or, in the case of persons on layoff, the average number of weeks since the termination of their most recent employment. This series is inversely related to broad movements in aggregate economic activity and vice-versa.

Exhibit 12-10

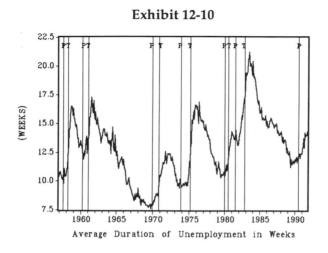

Average Duration of Unemployment in Weeks

INVENTORIES AND INVENTORY INVESTMENT

Ratio, Manufacturing and Trade Inventories to Sales in 1982 Dollars (77) (M,1 and 2) (Lg,Lg,Lg) measures the ratio of the end-of-month constant-dollar values of inventories on hand in the manufacturing, merchant wholesalers, and retail establishments to the constant-dollar value of monthly sales of these establishments. This series is computed by dividing series (70) by series (57) and expressing the result as a ratio. Series (70) measures the constant- dollar value of inventories held by manufacturing, merchant wholesalers, and retail establishments. The monthly volume of manufacturing, merchant wholesalers, and retail establishments in constant dollars is reflected in series (57).

Exhibit 12-11

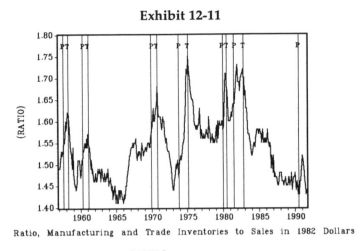

Ratio, Manufacturing and Trade Inventories to Sales in 1982 Dollars

PRICES, COSTS, AND PROFITS

Change in Index of Labor Cost Per Unit of Output, Mfg. (smoothed) (62) (M,1 and 4) (Lg,Lg,Lg) measures the relationship between the value of production of manufactured goods and the cost of the labor involved in that production. It is calculated by taking the ratio of the index of compensation of employees in manufacturing to the manufacturing component of the industrial production index and converting the resulting ratios to an index. This information is shown in index form and as a percent of the trend.

Exhibit 12-12

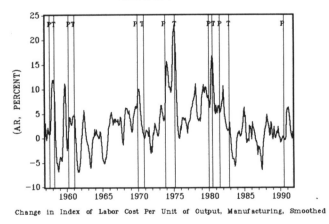

Change in Index of Labor Cost Per Unit of Output, Manufacturing, Smoothed

Change in Consumer Price Index for Services (smoothed) (120) (M,1 and 2) (Lg,Lg,Lg) is calculated by measuring the changes occurring in the CPI for services between reporting dates.

Exhibit 12-13

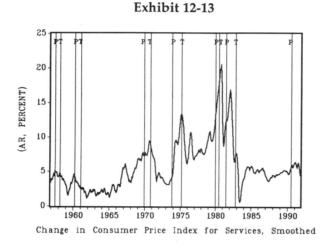

Change in Consumer Price Index for Services, Smoothed

MONEY AND CREDIT

Average Prime Rate Charged by Banks (109) (M,4) (Lg,Lg,Lg)
measures the interest rate banks charge their most credit-worthy customers for short-term loans. It is a rate used in determining the rates charged on most loans to other business customers. It is not as sensitive as money-market instrument rates such as T-Bills or the Fed Fund rates, which fluctuate daily. Its movements are less frequent and change in larger increments. It is calculated using the averages of reported rates of 30 large money-market banks.

Exhibit 12-14

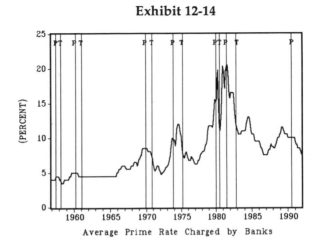

Average Prime Rate Charged by Banks

Commercial and Industrial Loans Outstanding—1982 Dollars (101) (M,1,4, and the Federal Reserve Bank of New York) (Lg,Lg,Lg) is a result of deflating series 72 Commercial and Industrial Loans Outstanding in Current Dollars using the Producer Price Index, All Commodities. Series 72 is computed by summing the following components:

1. Balances outstanding on loans for commercial and industrial purposes held or sold outright by large commercial banks (except loans secured by real estate), loans to financial institutions, and loans to purchase or carry securities.

2. Commercial paper issued by nonfinancial companies.

Exhibit 12-15

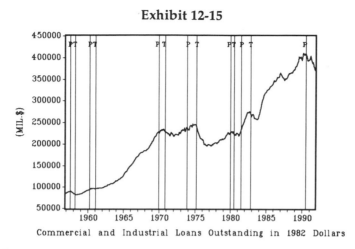

Commercial and Industrial Loans Outstanding in 1982 Dollars

Ratio, Consumer Installment Credit Outstanding to Personal Income (95) (M,1 and 2) (Lg,Lg,Lg) is an estimate of most short and intermediate credit used to purchase commodities and services for personal consumption or to refinance debts originally incurred for such a purpose. Credit extended to government agencies, nonprofit, or charitable organizations, farmers, businesses and industries for business purposes is excluded.

Exhibit 12-16

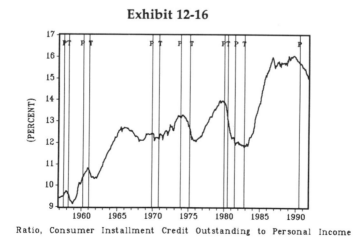

Ratio, Consumer Installment Credit Outstanding to Personal Income

CHAPTER 13

NATIONAL ECONOMIC MEASURES

Many different measures are available and they are quoted widely. Some measures are of a monthly nature while others are quarterly. Most measures are quarterly, and hence lack the timeliness of monthly measures. The National Income and Product Accounts (NIPAs) are also subject to revision as additional information that affects previous estimates and revisions becomes available. The latest major revision was in November 1991, and is described later.

PRICE MOVEMENTS

Two of the most awaited monthly indexes are those that measure the extent of inflation. Besides the indexes described here, there are other indexes which measure the individual component changes within the particular all-inclusive index.

Consumer Price Index for All Urban Consumers (320) (M,3)

Consumer Price Index measures the average change in the cost of a fixed market basket of goods and services purchased by consumers. These consumers, who comprise about 80 percent of the non-institutional population of the United States, include urban wage earners, clerical, professional, managerial, and technical workers, the self-employed, the unemployed, and retirees and others not in the labor force. The index excludes farm families, military personnel, and persons in institutions.

The index represents price changes for everything purchased by urban consumers—food, clothing, automobiles, homes, house furnishings, household supplies, fuel, drugs, and recreational goods, fees to doctors and lawyers, rent, repair costs, transportation fares, and public utility rates. Federal, state, and city taxes (sales, excise, real estate, etc.) directly associated with the purchase and continued ownership of an item are included in the price, but income, personal property, and social security taxes are not. Property taxes are included in the costs of home owner- ship and are implicitly included in rental cost. Prices are obtained by personal visits to stores and service establishments, chain and inde- pendent retail stores, professional people, and repair and service shops. Rental costs are obtained from tenants.

The quantity and quality of items contained in the market basket are held constant except at times of weight revisions. Therefore, CPIs reflect only changes in prices and none of the other factors that affect family living expenses, such as change in family composition, changes in the kinds and amounts of goods and services families buy, or the total amount families buy, or the total amount families spend for living. In calculating the index, price changes for the various items in each location are combined with weights that represent their importance in the spend- ing of their respective index population.

Exhibit 13-1

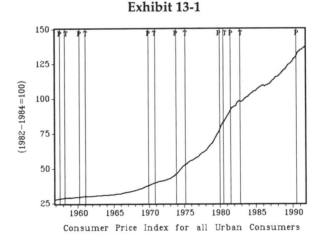

Consumer Price Index for all Urban Consumers

Producers' Price Index, Finished Goods (336). This index measures av- erage changes in prices received in primary markets in the United States (including Alaska and Hawaii) by producers of commodities at all stages of processing. They are designed to measure "pure" price changes; i.e., price changes not influenced by changes in quality, quantity, shipping terms, or produce mix.

The sample used to calculate these indexes contained about 2,800 commodities and 10,000 quotations per month, selected to represent the price movement of all commodities produced in the agriculture, forestry, fishing, mining, manufacturing, electric, gas, and other public utilities sectors. The universe includes crude, manufactured and processed goods produced in the United States and those imported for sale in commercial transactions in primary markets in the United States. Civilian goods normally purchased by the government and goods that compete with those made in the producing sector (such as waste paper and scrap materials) also are included. In addition, government sales of some commodities (e.g., electric power) are included if they are considered competitive with free market sales. Individually priced items (e.g., works of art), goods transferred between establishments owned by the same company, goods sold at retail by producer-owned retail establishments, and military goods are excluded.

Exhibit 13-2

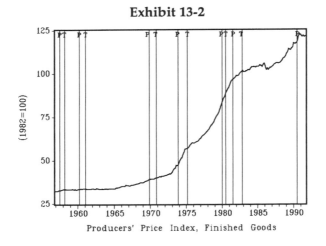

Producers' Price Index, Finished Goods

Notice that the producer price index has decreased at times, while the consumer price index just increases all the time. This probably due to what most have experienced, namely that if prices go up on a consumer level, they very seldom go down once producer prices have decreased. If both the CPI and the PPI are graphed together, the trend will become more apparent.

Exhibit 13-3

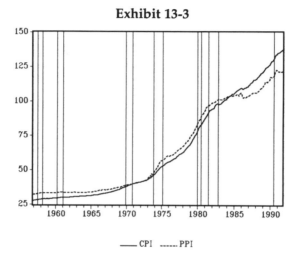

—— CPI ------ PPI

Implicit Price Deflator for Gross National Product (310) (Q,1) is a current weighted price index (1982 = 100), and is derived by dividing the current dollar GNP by the constant dollar GNP for each period. It is a weighted average of the detailed price indexes used in the deflation of GNP, with the composition of the constant dollar output in each quarter as weights. In other words, the price indexes for each quarter are weighted by the ratio of the quantity of the item valued in 1982 prices. Therefore, changes in the implicit price deflator reflect both changes in prices and in the composition of output.

This indicator may be adjusted in 1992 to reflect the new 1987 base year. Its use is a close proxy for a deflator for GDP, since there is no material difference in the two aggregates.

As an important feature of the November 1991 revision, alternative price and quantity indexes will be introduced. These will supply choices other than the present standard constant-dollar measures and other fixed weighted price indexes.

Exhibit 13-4

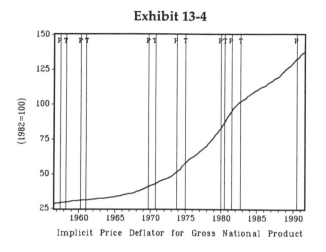

Implicit Price Deflator for Gross National Product

Fixed-Weighted Price Index for Gross Domestic Product (311) (Q,1)
will be an additional series supported in 1992.
    Data to be available in 1992.

NATIONAL INCOME AND PRODUCT ACCOUNTS

National economic measures are mainly concerned with the National Income and Product Accounts (NIPAs). These accounts are of a quarterly
nature. A comprehensive revision of the NIPAs was completed in November 1991. There have been a total of nine comprehensive revisions,
with the last prior revision released in December 1985. Parker (1991) defines a comprehensive revision as incorporating three kinds of changes,
namely definitional and classificational changes, statistical changes, and
new and redesigned tables. The most important apparent changes in this
revision are

- ■ a change in base year from 1982 to 1987,

- ■ a change in emphasis from Gross National Product (GNP) to
   Gross Domestic Product (GDP),

- ■ a change in the future from the present implicit price deflator
   to add a variable weight index. This new index would value
   GNP and GDP on more recent prices instead of on a fixed
   weight of the base year.

Changes in the base year require restatement of many of the series. Presently the revision is available only for 1959 to the current period. Additional restatements will be completed in 1992, and will go back to 1929 where required.

Framework for Understanding NIPAs

The following information is adapted from various selected National Income and Production Account (NIPA) tables prepared by the National Income and Wealth Division, Bureau of Economic Research (1990). Percentages are added to show individual influence upon certain measures. In looking over this exhibit, one should also be aware of the amounts representing large aggregate numbers from many different sources. This is one reason why the amounts are subject to revision.

Relationship of National Income and Product Accounts

		Year 1990 Billions of Dollars	%
Personal Consumption Expenditures		3,742.6	67.9
Durable Goods	465.9		
Nondurable Goods	1,217.7		
Services	2,059.0		
Gross Private Domestic Investment		802.7	14.6
Fixed Investment	802.7		
Change in Business Inventories	0.0		
Net Exports of Goods and Services		<74.4>	<1.4>
Exports	550.4		
Imports	<624.8>		
Government Purchase of Goods and Services		1,042.9	18.9
Federal	424.9		
State	618.0		
Gross Domestic Product		5,513.8	100.0

	Year 1990 Billions of Dollars	%
Plus: Receipts of Factor Income From Rest of World	147.7	2.6
Less: Payments of Factor Income to Rest of World	<137.0>	<2.5>
Gross **National Product**	5,524.5	100.0
Less: Capital Consumption Adjustment	<594.7>	<10.6>
Equals: **Net National Product**	4,929.8	89.4
Less: Indirect Business Taxes, etc.	<439.2>	<7.9>
Business Transfer Payment	<27.7>	<.5>
Statistical Discrepancy	<8.1>	<.2>
Plus: Subsidies Less Current Surplus of Government Enterprises	4.8	
Equals: **National Income**	4,459.6	80.8

		Year 1990 Billions of Dollars	%
Less: Corporate Profits with			
IVadj and CCA	319.0		
Net Interest	490.1		
Contribution for			
Social Insurance	501.7		
Wage Accruals, etc.	.1	<1,310.9>	<23.6>
Plus: Personal Interest			
Income	721.3		
Government Transfer			
Payments to Persons	661.7		
Personal Dividend			
Income	124.8		
Business Transfer			
Payments	23.2		

		Year 1990 Billions of Dollars	%
Arithmetic Discrepancy	.1	1,531.1	27.8
Equals: **Personal Income**		4,679.8	84.8
Less: Personal Tax and Nontax Payments		<621.0>	<11.2>
Equals: **Disposable Income**		4,058.8	73.6
Less: Personal Consumption Expenditures	3,742.6		<67.87>

Interest Paid by
       Consumers to
       Businesses
	107.5		<1.9>

Payments to Foreigners	2.1		<.2>
Equals: **Personal Saving**		206.6	3.7

GROSS DOMESTIC PRODUCT/GROSS NATIONAL PRODUCT

In 1991, Gross National Product (GNP) will be de-emphasized in favor of Gross Domestic Product (GDP). This change is being made because GDP is seen as a better measure of short-term monitoring and analysis of the U.S. economy. The change to GDP also facilitates comparison of economic activity in the United States with that in other countries. GDP has been adopted by many countries in an effort to move toward a set of international guidelines for economic accounting.

Gross Domestic Product (GDP) (Q,1) measures the value of goods and services produced by labor and property located in the United States. This labor or property can be supplied by U.S. residents or residents of other countries.

Exhibit 13-5

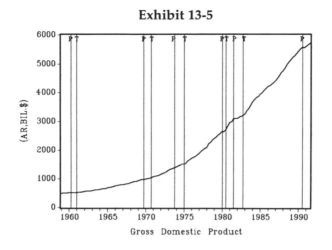

Gross Domestic Product

Gross Domestic Product in 1987 Dollars (Q,1) is derived by dividing components of the current-dollar GDP by appropriate price indexes in as fine a breakdown as possible.

Exhibit 13-6

Gross Domestic Product in 1987 Dollars

Gross National Product (GNP) was the most widely used measure of the nation's production. It measures the market value of the goods and services produced by the labor and property supplied by residents of the United States, whether located in the U.S. or abroad. More specifically, it is the market value of "final" sales of goods and services plus inventory change. Purchases by one producing unit from another of "intermediate" products are not included, but depreciation charges and other allowances for business and institutional consumption of fixed capital goods have not been deducted in deriving it.

GDP is measured as the sum of products:

> **Personal Consumption Expenditures (230)**
> **Gross Private Domestic Investment (240)**
> **Government Purchases of Goods and Services (260)**
> **Net Exports (Exports Less Imports) (250)**

GNP (200) (Q,1) can also be measured as the sum of the costs incurred and the profits earned in the production of the GNP.

Exhibit 13-7

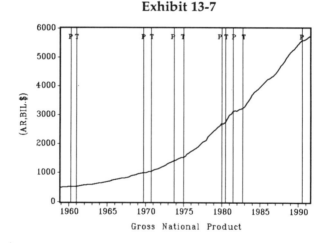

Gross National Product

Gross National Product in 1987 Dollars (50) (Q,1) (C,C,C) is derived by dividing components of the current-dollar GNP by appropriate price indexes in as fine a breakdown as possible.

Exhibit 13-8

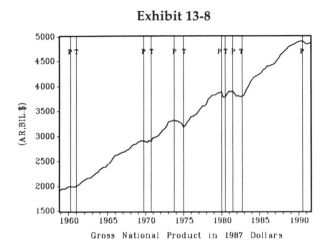

Gross National Product in 1987 Dollars

The differences between these two measures arise out of the payments received from the rest of the world or payments to the rest of the world. In 1990, these differences could be reconciled as follows:

	In Billions (1990 $'s)
GDP	$5,513.8
Plus Receipts from Rest of World	147.1
Less Payments to Rest of World	<137.0>
GNP	$5,524.5

This is a negligible difference in the case of the U.S. economy. Many countries have substantial foreign or rest-of-the-world investments. In those cases, GNP will be smaller than GDP because of the payments to the rest of the world.

PERSONAL CONSUMPTION EXPENDITURES

Personal Consumption Expenditures (PCE), a component of the Gross Domestic Product (GDP), is goods and services purchased by individuals, operating expenses of nonprofit institutions, and the value of food, fuel, clothing, rental of dwelling, and financial services received in kind by individuals. The estimated rental value of owner-occupied dwellings is included, but all private purchases of residential structures are classified as gross private domestic investment. PCE in 1987 dollars is obtained by dividing detailed components of current dollar PCE (series 230) by appropriate price indexes in as fine a breakdown as possible and summing the results using components of the Consumer Price Index for all Urban Consumers (CPI-U).

PCE is measured as the sum expended for:
Durable Goods
Nondurable Goods
Services

Total Personal Consumption Expenditures — Current Dollars (230).

Exhibit 13-9

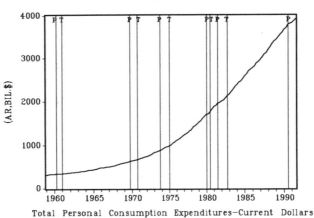

Total Personal Consumption Expenditures–Current Dollars

In current dollars, expenditures have increased steadily.

Total Personal Consumption Expenditures in 1987 Dollars (231) (Q,1)
is series **230 deflated.**

Exhibit 13-10

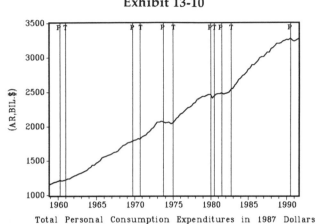

Total Personal Consumption Expenditures in 1987 Dollars

Total Durable Goods in Current Dollars (232) (Q,1) represents a component of **Personal Consumption Expenditures (230).**

Exhibit 13-11

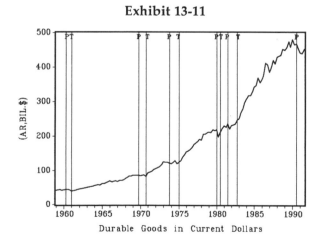

Durable Goods in Current Dollars

Total durable goods has an increasing long-term trend, but its progress
is more erratic than that of nondurable goods.

Total Durable Goods in 1987 Dollars (233) (Q,1) is series **232 deflated.**

Exhibit 13-12

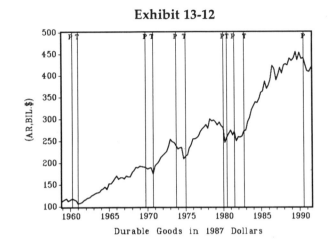

Durable Goods in 1987 Dollars

Nondurable Goods in Current Dollars (236) (Q,1) represents a component of **Personal Consumption Expenditures (230).**

Exhibit 13-13

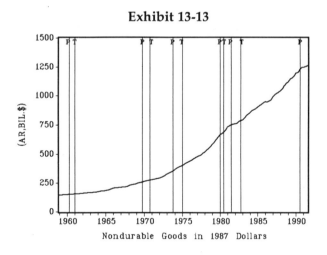

Nondurable Goods in 1987 Dollars

Nondurable Goods in 1987 Dollars (238) (Q,1) is series **236 deflated.**

Exhibit 13-14

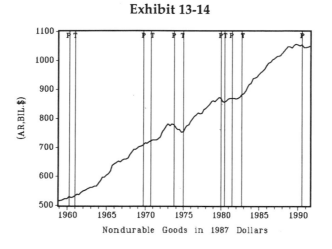

Nondurable Goods in 1987 Dollars

The percentage change in nondurable goods is much less than that of durable goods.

Services in Current Dollars (237) (Q,1) represents a component of **Personal Consumption Expenditures (230).**

Exhibit 13-15

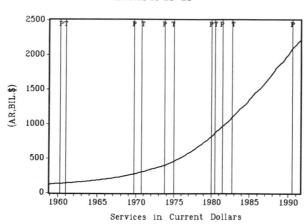

Services in Current Dollars

Services in 1987 Dollars (239) (Q,1) is series 237 deflated.

Exhibit 13-16

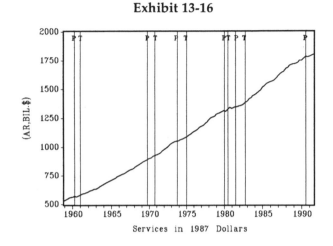

Services in 1987 Dollars

Service-sector expenditures have expanded steadily, as seen at peaks and troughs. In 1990 and 1991, the service-sector expenditures seemed to be more sensitive to the recession.

GROSS PRIVATE DOMESTIC INVESTMENT

Gross Private Domestic Investment (GPDI), a component of the Gross Domestic Product (GDP), is fixed capital goods purchased by private businesses and nonprofit institutions, and the value of the changes in the physical value of inventories held by private businesses. GPDI includes all private purchases of dwellings. The constant dollar (1987 dollars) is derived principally by dividing component price indexes and summing the results.

Total Gross Private Domestic Investment in Current Dollars (240) (Q,1).

Exhibit 13-17

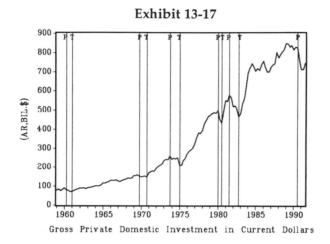

Gross Private Domestic Investment in Current Dollars

Total Gross Private Domestic Investment in 1987 Dollars (241) (Q,1).

Exhibit 13-18

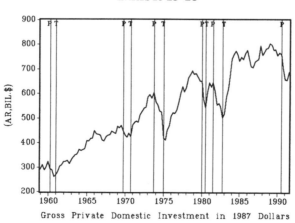

Gross Private Domestic Investment in 1987 Dollars

Material changes can be noted at peaks and troughs.

Gross Private Domestic Fixed Investment — Current Dollars (242) (Q,1) is a component of **Gross Private Domestic Investment (240)**.

Exhibit 13-19

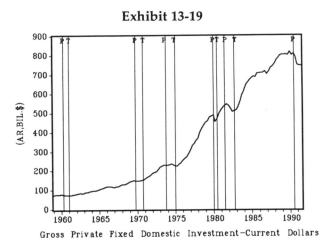

Gross Private Fixed Domestic Investment–Current Dollars

Gross Private Domestic Fixed Investment — 1987 Dollars (243) (Q,1) is series **242 deflated.**

Exhibit 13-20

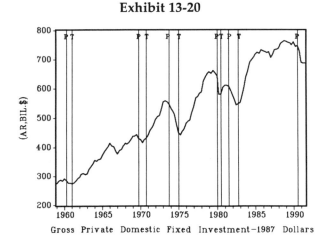

Gross Private Domestic Fixed Investment–1987 Dollars

Gross fixed investment is the largest component of the gross domestic investment.

Change in Business Inventories in Current Dollars (245) (Q,1) is a component of **Gross Private Domestic Investment (240).**

Exhibit 13-21

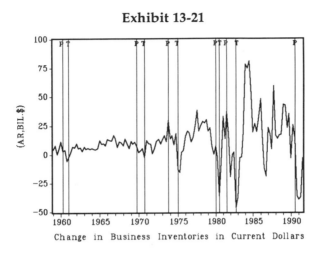

Change in Business Inventories in Current Dollars

Change in Business Inventories in 1987 Dollars (30) (Q,1) (L,L,L) is series **245 deflated.**

Exhibit 13-22

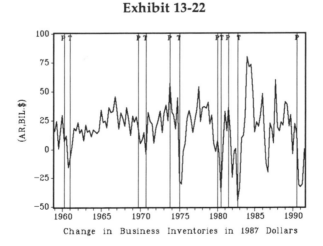

Change in Business Inventories in 1987 Dollars

The using and rebuilding of inventories at peaks and troughs are easily visualized using this change series.

GOVERNMENT PURCHASES OF GOODS AND SERVICES

Government Purchases of Goods and Services is a component of GDP, and the Federal Component is based essentially on the *Monthly Statement of Receipts and Outlays of the U.S. Government* issued by the U.S. Department of the Treasury. The state and local purchases of goods and services are derived from reports of the Government Division, and they are compiled by the Construction Statistics Division of the U.S. Department of Commerce, Bureau of Labor Statistics. Adjustments are made for items other than purchases of goods or services to reflect the proper GNP component. Different methods for deflating to constant dollars are used in an effort to match the appropriate deflator to the particular component.

Total Government Purchases of Goods and Services in Current Dollars (260) (Q,1) represents the total purchases of federal, state, and local government.

Exhibit 13-23

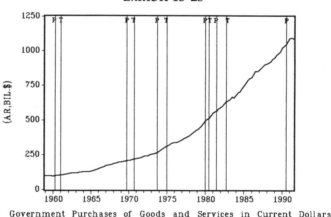

Government Purchases of Goods and Services in Current Dollars

Total Government Purchases of Goods and Services — 1987 Dollars (261) (Q,1) is series 260 deflated.

Exhibit 13-24

Total Government Purchases of Goods and Services–1987 Dollars

SIGNIFICANCE

Purchases have decreased or increased only slightly in constant dollars during contraction periods. Notice that this is in opposition to priming of the pump or increasing government purchases during recession. Possible implications for the future include the improbability of larger deficits since the present accumulated deficits are so great.

Federal Government Purchases of Goods and Services in Current Dollars (262) (Q,1) is a component of Total Government Purchases of Goods and Services (260).

Exhibit 13-25

Federal Government Purchases of Goods and Services—Current

Federal Government Purchases of Goods and Services — 1987 Dollars (263) (Q,1) is series **262** deflated.

Exhibit 13-26

Federal Government Purchases of Goods and Services—1987 Dollars

State and Local Government Purchases of Goods and Services — Current Dollars (266) (Q,1) is a component of **Total Government Purchases of Goods and Services (260).**

Exhibit 13-27

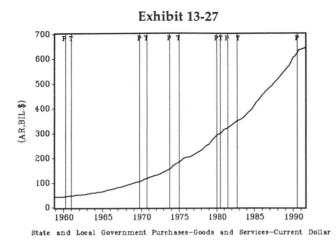

State and Local Government Purchases–Goods and Services–Current Dollar

State and Local Government Purchases of Goods and Services — 1987 Dollars (267) (Q,1) is series 266 deflated.

Exhibit 13-28

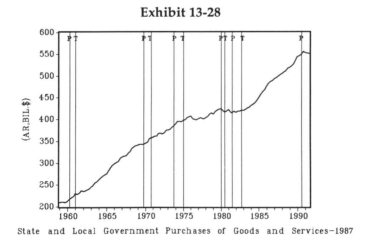

State and Local Government Purchases of Goods and Services–1987

Total government, federal government, and state and local government have all shown almost uninterrupted increases in spending.

NET EXPORTS OF GOODS AND SERVICES

Net Exports of Goods and Services, a component of Gross National Product (GNP), is exports less imports of goods and services. appropriate deflators are used to compute the constant dollars value. Specific trade unit value indexes are used for merchandise trade, and various other indexes are used for remaining components. The net exports in current dollars is a result of using series 252 (exports) and subtracting series 253 (imports). For constant dollars, series 255 is a result of subtracting series 257 from series 256.

Net Exports of Goods and Services in Current Dollars (250) (Q,1).

Exhibit 13-29

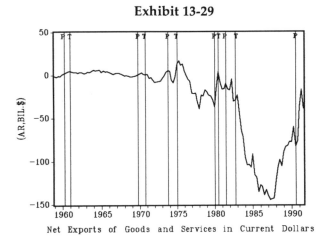

Net Exports of Goods and Services in Current Dollars

Net Exports of Goods and Services in 1987 Dollars (255) (Q,1) is series 250 deflated.

Exhibit 13-30

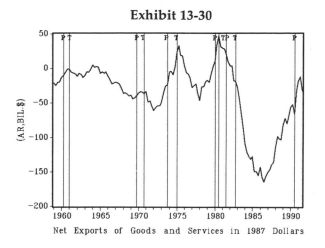

Net Exports of Goods and Services in 1987 Dollars

Exports of Goods and Services in Current Dollars (252) (Q,1) is a component **of Net Exports (210).**

Exhibit 13-31

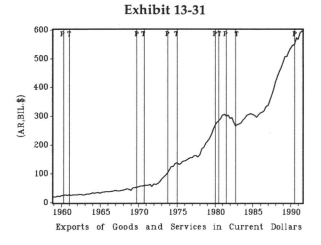

Exports of Goods and Services in Current Dollars

Exports of Goods and Services in 1987 Dollars (256) (Q,1) is series **252** deflated.

Exhibit 13-32

Exports of Goods and Services in 1987 Dollars

DISCUSSION

Foreign exchange rates have played an important part in determining large increases or decreases in exports.

Imports of Goods and Services in Current Dollars (253) (Q,1) is a component of **Net Exports (250).**

Exhibit 13-33

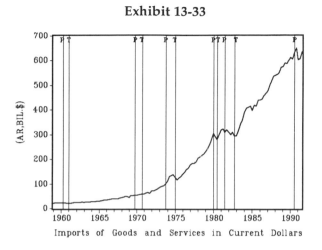

Imports of Goods and Services in Current Dollars

Imports of Goods and Services in 1987 Dollars (257) (Q,1) is series **253** deflated.

Exhibit 13-34

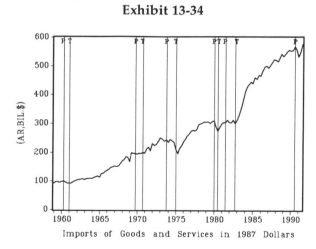

Imports of Goods and Services in 1987 Dollars

NATIONAL INCOME

National income is the income that originates in the production of goods and services attributable to labor and property supplied by residents of the United States. Incomes are recorded in the form in which they accrue to residents and are measured before taxes on those incomes. They consist of Compensation of Employees (280), Proprietors' Income (282), Rental Income (284), Corporate Profits (286), and Net Interest (288). The total represents Gross National Product less Capital Consumption Adjustment and Indirect Business Taxes.

Components of National Income
1990

	In Billions of Dollars
Compensation of Employees	3,290.3
Proprietors' Income with CCAdj and INN	373.2
Rental Income	-12.9
Corporate Profits with Adjustment	319.0
Net Interest	490.1
Rounding, Statistical Discrepancy	-.1
National Income	4,459.6

National Income in Current Dollar (220) (Q,1) is the aggregate measure.

Exhibit 13-35

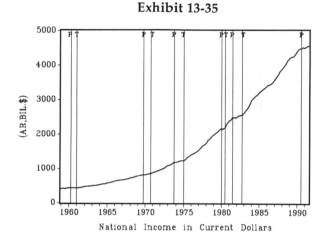

National Income in Current Dollars

Compensation of Employees (280) (Q,1) is one of the largest components of National Income.

Exhibit 13-36

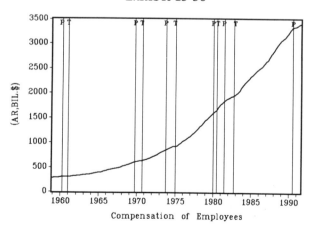

Compensation of Employees

Proprietors' Income with the IVA and CCAdj (282) (Q,1).

Exhibit 13-37

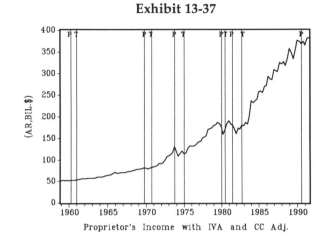

Proprietor's Income with IVA and CC Adj.

Corporate Profits Before Tax with IVA and CCAdj (286) (Q,1).

Exhibit 13-38

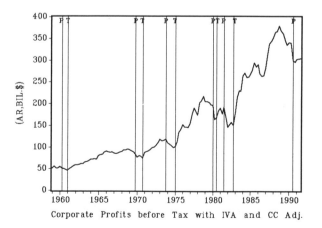

Corporate Profits before Tax with IVA and CC Adj.

SIGNIFICANCE

The profit and income components are subject to much greater variation than compensation of employees. Corporate profits are a much smaller component of national income than most people realize.

Net Interest (288) (Q,1).

Exhibit 13-39

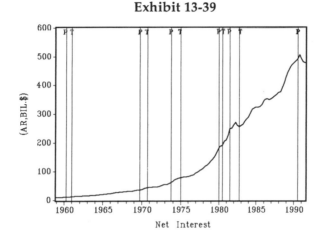

Net Interest

SAVING

Gross saving measures private saving (business and personal savings) plus government surplus or deficit.

Gross Saving (290) (Q,1) is the sum of business and personal saving plus government surpluses or deficits.

Exhibit 13-40

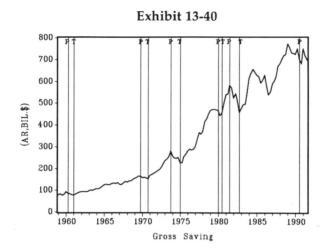

Gross Saving

Business Saving (295) (Q,1) consists of undistributed corporate profits plus corporate and noncorporate capital consumption allowances with CCAdj, plus corporate and noncorporate IVA, plus wage accruals less disbursements.

Exhibit 13-41

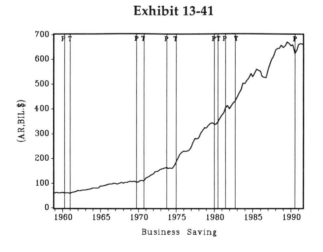

Business Saving

Personal Saving (292) (Q,1). Personal saving is personal income less personal outlays and personal tax and nontax payments. It is the current saving of individuals. Personal saving equals the change in the net worth of a person, which may also be viewed as the sum of net acquisition of financial assets and physical assets, less the sum of net borrowings and of capital consumption allowances, with capital consumption adjustment.

Exhibit 13-42

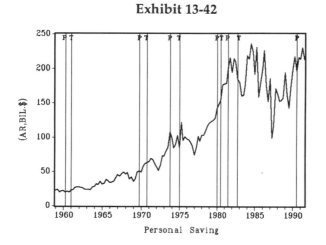

Personal Saving

Business saving is greater than personal saving and gives some indication of amounts available for future investment.

Government Surplus or Deficit (298) (Q,1) measures the difference between government receipts and government expenditures as recorded in the national income and product accounts. It also may be viewed as the net acquisition of financial assets by government and government enterprises, and net government purchases of land and of rights to government-owned land, including oil resources. Federal, state, and local governments are included in this series. The series is computed by adding the federal surplus or deficit (series 500) to the state and local government surplus and deficit (series 510).

Exhibit 13-43

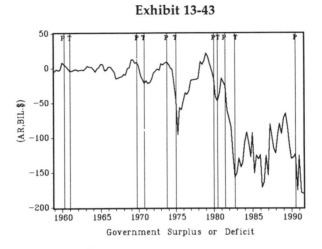

Government Surplus or Deficit

Personal Saving Rate (293) (Q,1) measures the portion of disposable personal income (224) that is saved (292). This series is computed by dividing series 292 by series 224 and expressing the resulting ratios as a percent.

Exhibit 13-44

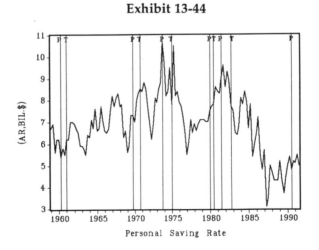

Personal Saving Rate

DISPOSABLE PERSONAL INCOME

Personal income is the income received by persons from all sources, that is, from participation in production, from transfer payments from government and business, and from government interest, which is treated like a transfer payment.

Transfer payments to persons are income payments to persons for which they do not render current services. Examples of business transfer payment include liability payments for personal injuries, corporate gifts to nonprofit institutions, and bad debts incurred by consumers. Government transfer payments include such items as social security, state unemployment, and payments to nonprofit institutions for work other than research and development.

Disposable personal income measures the personal income that is available for spending or saving. It is equal to personal income less personal tax and nontax payments. Personal taxes include income, estate and gift, and personal property taxes. Nontax payments include passport fees, fines, penalties, donations, tuition, and fees paid to schools and hospitals operated mainly by the government.

Disposable Personal Income in Current Dollars (224) (Q,1).

Exhibit 13-45

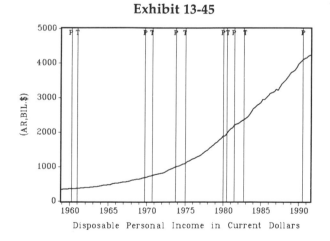

Disposable Personal Income in Current Dollars

Disposable Personal Income in Constant 1987 Dollars (225) (Q,1) is series 224 deflated.

Exhibit 13-46

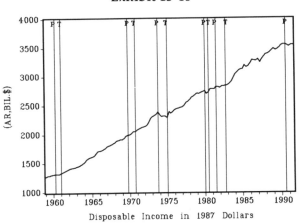

Disposable Income in 1987 Dollars

CHAPTER 14

INTERNATIONAL MEASURES AND COMPARISONS

Physically the world is the same size as in previous centuries. The distance from one nation to another has not changed, but the rapid increase in the speed at which communication can take place has shrunk the effects of distance dramatically. Now, the action of one government or large multinational organization can be addressed almost immediately by other affected governments or businesses. No longer does mere physical distance isolate and allow resistance to changing conditions outside a national boundary.

In examining international measures, one finds many different organizations which are concerned with the collection of data and its distribution. Most of the organizations are of a quasi-governmental character, with the membership being composed of individual nations. These organizations publish a variety of informative literature, ranging from monthly magazines to yearly handbooks to special studies on matters of concern. In most cases, information can be accessed through a number of database organizations previously discussed. Some of the organizations from which data and information are available are as follows:

Organization of Economic Cooperation and Development (OECD) was established in 1961 and has the following aims:

- to encourage growth and maintain financial stability in member firms by developing, coordinating and promoting policies,

- to coordinate efforts of member firms in providing financial and technical aid to developing countries, and

■   to develop and co-ordinate expansion of trade.

Membership in the OECD includes most industrialized countries.

United Nations (UN) is the largest single organization of member nations. Most parties associate the UN with peacekeeping, but its activities are diverse. A literature search could disclose particular information available, that could be relevant to a particular area of interest.

International Monetary Fund (IMF) was formed in 1944. Its membership is composed of most of the non-Communist countries. It would seem that this membership will be greatly increased as the previously Communist countries convert to other forms of government. The primary purpose of the fund is to provide a reserve of foreign exchange on which member governments may draw during temporary balance-of-payments difficulties. This organization publishes the monthly *International Financial Statistics*, which provides a country's financial information to member firms and others.

DATA ANALYSIS

Once data is gathered and available for use, it must be analyzed to ascertain its particular attributes, and hence its uses. Geoffrey Moore in his book *International Economic Indicators: A Sourcebook* describes the methods and procedures by which data is studied and measures developed.

The Center for International Business Cycle Research (CIBCR), with which Geoffrey Moore is associated, has developed and maintains a continuing interest in international indicators. Their monthly publication *International Economic Indicators* describes their service and area of interest as follows:

> provides a monthly look at 169 economic series covering
> 11 industrial countries (96 of these series are unavailable
> from any other source).

Time series research resulted in the development of indicators using the methodology described previously for selecting and evaluating indicators in the U.S. economy.

CIBCR has developed composite leading and coincident indexes for 11 industrial countries and for groups of countries. Their literature states that the indexes have been shown to be useful in forecasting and interpreting fluctuations in output, employment, inflation, interest rates, and foreign trade. All indexes with source of CIBCR are reproduced with permission of CIBCR, the copyright holder.

Group of Seven Leading Index (M, CIBCR) is a composite index of the Group of Seven countries, namely, U.S., U.K., France, Germany, Italy, Japan, and Canada.

Exhibit 14-1

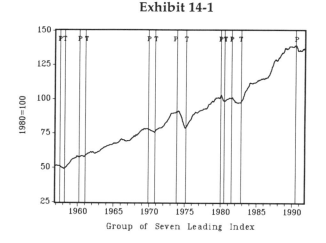

Group of Seven Leading Index

The components of the leading index vary according to the particular country's series, but the content seems similar in the economic process found to be significant. The components of this Leading Index for the Group of Seven follow in Table 14-1.

Table 14-1

LEADING INDEX COMPONENTS

ECONOMIC PROCESS/INDICATOR	COUNTRY
I. Employment and Unemployment	
Average Workweek, Mfg. (hrs. per week)	U.S., U.K., Canada, France
Number of Working Short Hours	Germany
Hours per Month per Worker in Industry	Italy
Index of Overtime Worked — Mfg.	Japan
Initial Claims, Unemployment Insurance	U.S., Canada
Applications for Unemployment Compensation (inverted)	Germany
New Unemployment Claims (inverted)	France
II. Fixed Capital Investment	
New Business Formation	U.S.
New Companies Registered	U.K.
Contracts and Orders, Plant and Equipment	U.S.
New Orders, Machinery and Equipment	Canada
New Orders, Engineering Industries	U.K.
New Orders, Investment Goods Industries	Germany
New Orders for Machinery and Construction Work	Japan
New Building Permits, Private Housing Units	U.S.
Nonresidential Building Permits	Canada
Residential Building Permits	Canada, France
Construction, New Orders Private Industry	U.K.
Housing Starts	U.K.
Residential Construction Orders in Constant Prices	Germany
Dwelling Units Started	Japan
Business Failures	U.K.
Insolvent Enterprises	Germany
Declared Bankruptcies	Italy
III. Inventory and Inventory Investment	
Change in Business Inventories	U.S.
Change in Inventories	Germany, Japan
Change in Stocks and Work in Progress	U.K.

Table 14-1 (Continued)

ECONOMIC PROCESS/INDICATOR	COUNTRY
Change in Nonfarm Business Inventories	Canada
Change in Stocks	France
IV. Orders and Deliveries	
New Orders, Consumer Goods and Materials	U.S.
New Orders, Consumer Goods	Canada
Change in Unfilled Orders	France, Italy
V. Prices, Costs, and Profits	
Change in Industrial Materials Prices	U.S.
Change in Basic Materials Prices (percent)	U.K., Germany
Change in Imported Raw Materials Prices	France
Change in Imported Industrial Materials Prices	Italy
Stock Prices	U.S., U.K., Canada, Japan, Germany, Italy
Corporate Profits After Taxes	U.S., U.K., Canada
Gross Entrepreneurial and Property Income	Germany
Ratio, Price to Unit Labor Cost, Nonfarm Business	U.S.
Ratio, Price to Unit Labor Cost	U.K., Canada, Germany, Italy, Japan

Group of Seven Coincident Index (M, CIBCR) is a composite index of the Group of Seven countries, namely U.S., U.K., France, Germany, Italy, Japan, and Canada.

Exhibit 14-2

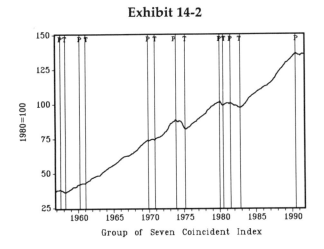

Group of Seven Coincident Index

The components of the coincident index vary according to the particular country's series, but the content seems similar to the economic process found to be significant. The components of this Coincident Index for the Group of Seven follow in Table 14-2.

Table 14-2

COINCIDENT INDICATORS

ECONOMIC PROCESSING/INDICATOR	COUNTRY
I. National Income and Product	
Personal Income	U.S., Canada
Gross Domestic Product	U.S., U.K., Canada, France, Germany, Italy
Gross National Expenditures	Japan
Personal Disposable Income	U.K.
Wage and Salary Income in Constant Prices	Japan
II. Employment and Unemployment	
Nonfarm Employment	U.S.
Employment in Production Industries	U.K., Germany
Employment in Mining and Manufacturing	Germany
Regular Workers Employment, All Industries	Japan
Unemployment Rate (Percent Inverted)	U.S., U.K., Canada, Italy, Germany, Japan
Registered Unemployment	France
III. Consumption, Trade Orders, and Deliveries	
Industrial Production	U.S., U.K., Canada, France, Germany, Italy, Japan
Manufacturing and Trade Sales	U.S.
Retail Sales	U.K., Canada, France
Manufacturing Sales	Germany
Retail Trade	Germany
Retail Sales in Constant Prices	Italy, Japan

Additional leading and coincident indicators are available through CIBCR by country or by specialized groupings, i.e., Five Pacific Region Countries, Four European Countries, etc.

There are many individual indicators and measures, with some of the most commonly quoted dealing with gross domestic product, industrial production, consumer prices, stock prices, and foreign-exchange rates.

GROSS DOMESTIC PRODUCT

Gross Domestic Product (GDP) measures the production and income growth inside national borders. Foreign capital at work in industry inside a nation's borders is included, while receipts from investments abroad are excluded. The U.S. has made the change to an emphasis on GDP instead of on the more familiar comprehensive GNP in the 1991 third quarter. Restatements for the U.S. have been made from the first quarter of 1959 through the third quarter of 1991. Restatements for prior years will be available in 1992.

The graphs use figures denominated in each nation's local currency. The size of each nation's economy can best be analyzed by a comparison of its economy to that of other nations.

Gross Domestic Product reduced to dollar terms is shown below with the respective percent of the total.

GROSS DOMESTIC PRODUCT

Group of Seven

	1988 (Bil. $)	%
United States	4,881.0	40.9
Canada	471.8	4.0
United Kingdom	801.6	6.7
Germany	1,213.0	10.2
France	920.0	7.7
Italy	796.5	6.6
Japan	2,856.0	26.9
	11,939.9	100.0

CANADA, Gross Domestic Product (IMF,Q)

Exhibit 14-3

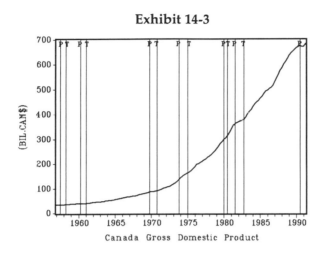

Canada Gross Domestic Product

UNITED KINGDOM, Gross Domestic Product (IMF,Q).

Exhibit 14-4

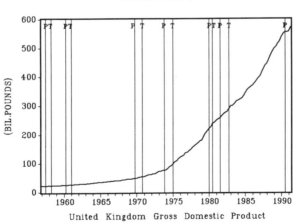

United Kingdom Gross Domestic Product

FEDERAL REPUBLIC OF GERMANY, Gross National Product (IMF,Q)

Exhibit 14-5

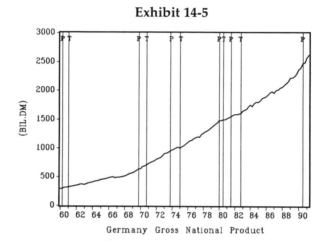

Germany Gross National Product

FRANCE, Gross Domestic Product (IMF,Q)

Exhibit 14-6

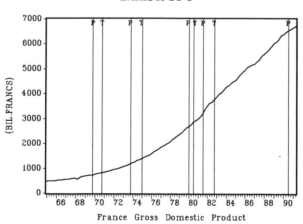

France Gross Domestic Product

ITALY, Gross Domestic Product (IMF,Q)

Exhibit 14-7

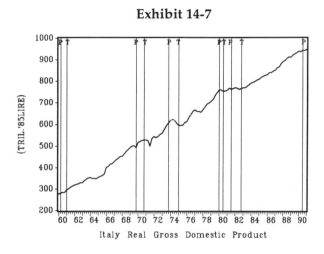

Italy Real Gross Domestic Product

JAPAN, Gross National Expenditure (IMF,Q)

Exhibit 14-8

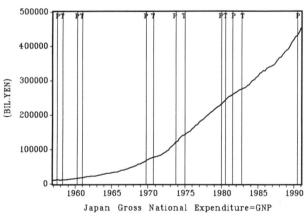

Japan Gross National Expenditure=GNP

INDUSTRIAL PRODUCTION

The level of industrial production has always been a good indicator of expectations to employment and profits. The United States is a major market for much of the world's goods. A comparison of the United States' Index of Industrial Production, Series 47, with other national indicators shows some remarkable visual similarities. In some cases, the peaks and troughs of business cycles and the resultant expansion and contraction of industrial production are almost mirror images.

Indexes of industrial production measure changes in value added by industrial activity expressed in constant prices. The weights used to comprise the index are generally proportionate to the industry's value added at factor cost and are determined from industrial census data for each nation.

To facilitate comparison, industrial production indexes are converted to a 1967=100 base by the U.S. Department of Commerce, Bureau of Economic Analysis. These series are seasonally adjusted.

CANADA, Index of Industrial Production (723). This index covers mining, manufacturing, and electric power, gas, and water utilities. The industries surveyed accounted for about 30 percent of gross domestic product at factor cost in 1971.

Exhibit 14-9

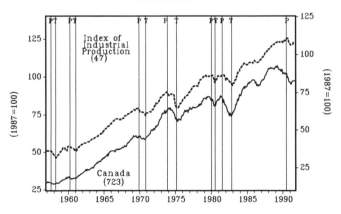

Source: Statistics Canada (Ottawa)

UNITED KINGDOM, Index of Industrial Production (722). This index covers mining, manufacturing (excluding slaughtering, fish curing, packaging by wholesalers, milk bottling without processing, custom tailoring, dressmaking, automobile, musical instruments, jewelry, and other repair work), electricity, gas, and water.

Exhibit 14-10

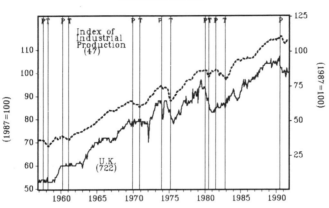

Source: Central Statistical Office (London)

FEDERAL REPUBLIC OF GERMANY, Index of Industrial Production (725). This index covers mining, manufacturing, construction, electricity, and gas. This sample accounted for 77 percent of industrial value added in 1970.

Exhibit 14-11

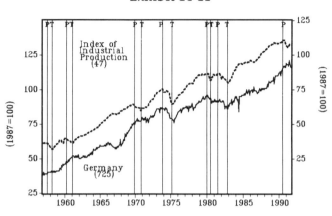

Source: Statistisches Bundesamt (Wiesbaden)

FRANCE, Index of Industrial Production (726). This index includes mining, manufacturing (excluding food and beverages, clothing, wood and wood products, nonelectrical machinery, aircraft, and certain other miscellaneous manufactures), electricity, and gas.

Exhibit 14-12

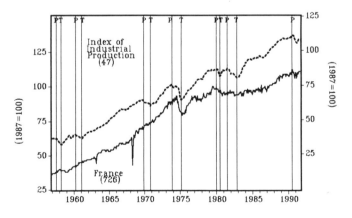

Source: Institut National de la Statistique et des Etudes Economiques (Paris)

ITALY, Index of Industrial Production (727). This index covers mining, manufacturing (except photographic equipment, magnetic tapes, and disks), electricity, and gas. The industrial divisions represented in the index accounted for 93 percent of industrial value added in 1970.

Exhibit 14-13

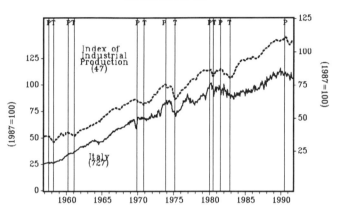

Source: Istituto Centrale di Statistica (Rome)

JAPAN, Index of Industrial Production (728). This index covers mining, manufacturing (excluding printing and publishing), electricity, and gas.

Exhibit 14-14

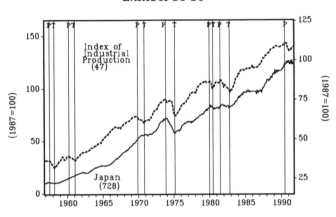

Source: Ministry of International Trade and Industry (Tokyo)

DISCUSSION

It would be interesting to compare the indexes for the purpose of finding out whether the index might be a reliable indicator of possible changes in another country.

CONSUMER PRICES

Inflation has always been present in most economies. Its range varies from an acceptable 3 percent to the unacceptable double-digit inflation rates experienced in the United States in the 1970s. Government intervention to control inflation is generally always present. The abilities of nations to control inflation differ dramatically. The Consumer Price Index (CPI) for all urban consumers (320) was plotted against the applicable national measure to provide some visual comparison of its ability as compared to the United States'. In most instances the greatest increases in inflation occurred at the same times in the various countries.

Consumer price indexes measure changes in the cost of selected goods and services that are considered representative of the consumption patterns of the particular country. The price indexes of the components are weighted to take account of the importance of each item in the expenditures of the population covered in the index. The weights usually are determined from family expenditure surveys taken in selected years. Where surveys are not conducted, consumption expenditures from the national income and product accounts are used to estimate the weights. Retail prices of goods and the cost of services are generally collected at regular intervals from retail and service outlets located in areas covered by the index. The base year and the method of computation vary among countries. To facilitate comparison, the indexes shown in BCD have been converted to a 1967=100 base by the U.S. Department of Commerce, International Trade Administration.

CANADA, Consumer Price Index (733). Items included in this index are food, housing (measured by rent, home ownership, including repairs and maintenance, fuel and light, and other household operation), clothing, transportation, health and personal care, recreation, education, reading, tobacco and alcoholic beverages. The prices of the majority of items are collected monthly. Rent quotations are obtained through monthly household surveys currently covering approximately 10,500 rented dwellings in urban areas No account is taken of seasonal fluctuations of items priced.

Exhibit 14-15

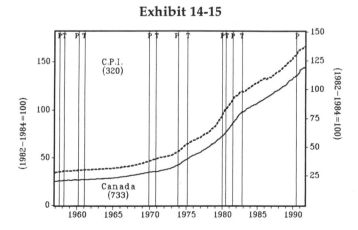

Source: Statistics Canada (Ottawa)

UNITED KINGDOM, Consumer Price Index (732). Items included in this index are food (including take-out food), alcoholic beverages, tobacco, housing (measured by rent, owner-occupied mortgage interest payments, insurance of dwelling, repairs and maintenance, taxes and water charges), fuel and light, clothing, durable household goods, transportation and vehicles, miscellaneous goods and services.

Exhibit 14-16

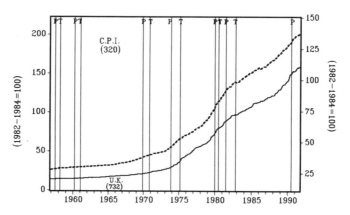

Source: Department of Employment (London)

FEDERAL REPUBLIC OF GERMANY, Consumer Price Index (735). Items included in this index are food, tobacco, clothing, rent, fuel and light, household operation, transportation, communications, health and personal care, education, entertainment, and other goods and services. Most prices are collected near the middle of each month in 118 municipalities. Between May and October, prices for fresh fruits and vegetables are collected twice a month. Rent quotations cover two- or three-room flats with kitchens and are obtained quarterly. In the computation of the index, seasonal fluctuations are taken into account for prices of items subject to such fluctuations.

Exhibit 14-17

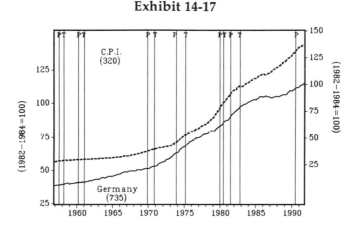

Source: Statistisches Bundesamt (Wiesbaden)

FRANCE, Consumer Price Index (736). Items included in this index are food, tobacco, clothing and household linen, furnishings, household goods, cleaning materials, fuel and light, and services (rent, water, maintenance and repairs, personal medical care, public transport and maintenance of vehicles, and other services).

Exhibit 14-18

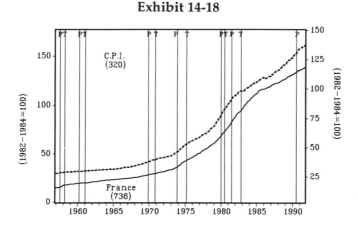

Source: Institut National de la Statistique et des Etudes Economiques (Paris)

ITALY, Consumer Price Index (737). Items included in this index are food, tobacco, rent, fuel, and light, clothing, furnishings and household equipment, personal and medical care, transportation, communication, education, recreation, and miscellaneous.

Exhibit 14-19

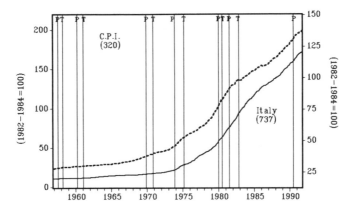

Source: Instituto Centrale di Statistica (Rome)

JAPAN, Consumer Price Index (738). Items included in this index are food, housing (rent, repairs and improvements, water charge, furniture and utensils), fuel and light, clothing, and miscellaneous.

Exhibit 14-20

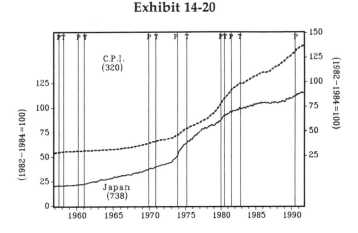

Source: Bureau of Statistics, Office of the Prime Minister (Tokyo)

DISCUSSION

Rates of change can be constructed from the previous indexes and could result in showing the differences between one country and another in a more apparent and effective manner. These changes in percent are available for the measures presented. Also, in the period between 1975 and 1980 the indexes increased sharply, signifying events of international importance that affect all the economies of the world. It was during this period that the price of oil increased dramatically, influencing most oil costs throughout the world.

STOCK PRICES

Stock prices in the United States have been a leading indicator of business cycle turning points. In the years following WW II, the United States has been a banker to the rest of the world. Currently, the United States still represents one of the largest individual free national marketplaces for money. With no capital transfer restrictions and a stable political environment, investors of other countries have looked upon the U.S. as a safe haven.

Stock price indexes are designed to approximate the average movement of stock prices on the individual country's leading exchange. Each stock included in the index must represent a viable enterprise and must be representative of the industry group to which it is assigned. The index estimates the change in value accruing to a hypothetical investor who, in the base period, bought shares corresponding in selection and proportions to those in the index (only substituted new issues for retired issues; and retained, in the form of shares, the proceeds of all offered rights, warrants, and share dividends). The base year and method of computation vary among countries. To facilitate comparison, the stock price indexes shown in BCD have been converted to a 1967=100 base by the U.S. Department of Commerce, Bureau of Economic Analysis. Current users should check the particular indexes, as their content is subject to revision.

CANADA, Index of Stock Prices (743). This index is a weighted index of 65 industrial stocks traded on at least one exchange. It has a 1971 reference base and is a component of the Investors Index. Prior to 1974, stocks traded on the Canadian Stock Exchange (CSE) also were included in 1974 because CSE merged with the Montreal Stock Exchange. Prices for component stocks are combined into subgroups in proportion to the relative numbers of shares outstanding as of January 1st each year. Each subgroup and group is weighted by its average yearly volume of shares traded over the period 1971-74. Adjustments are made to reflect changes in portfolio composition and stock splits.

Exhibit 14-21

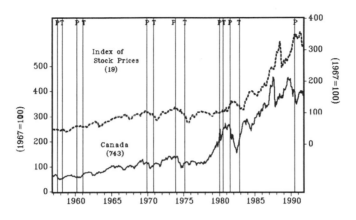

Source: Toronto Stock Exchange (Toronto)

UNITED KINGDOM, Index of Stock Prices (742). This index measures the monthly average of daily changes in the market value of a portfolio of 500 ordinary stocks actively traded on the London Exchange and issued by industrial companies operating in the United Kingdom. The sample, which is reviewed regularly, was originally comprised of all companies whose market capitalization in 1962 exceeded 4 million pounds; a few smaller companies also are included. Companies operating mainly outside the United Kingdom are excluded. In 1962, about 60 percent of all quoted industrial stocks were covered.

Exhibit 14-22

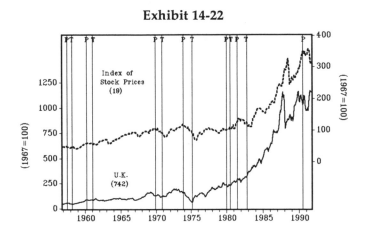

Source: Central Statistical Office (London)

FEDERAL REPUBLIC OF GERMANY, Index of Stock Prices (745). This index measures price changes in common stocks of companies with headquarters in Germany. It is comprised of 192 companies that represent approximately 90 percent of total authorized capital. Selection is based on the amount of authorized capital, with some adjustments to include small companies that influence the movements of the stock price index.

Exhibit 14-23

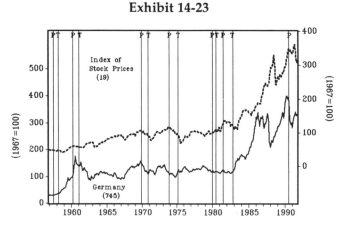

Source: Statisches Bundesamt (Wiesbaden)

FRANCE, Index of Stock Prices (746). This index measures monthly changes in the price of a portfolio of variable-yield industrial stocks admitted to the Paris Exchange. The sample of approximately 180 stocks is updated each year, with selection based on the market value of shares capital and the volume of transactions.

Exhibit 14-24

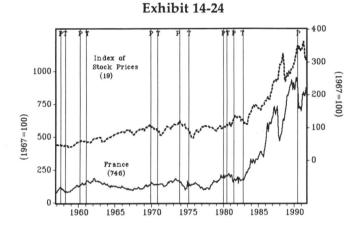

Source: Institut National de la Statistique et des etudes Economiques (Paris)

ITALY, Index of Stock Prices (747). This index measures the monthly averages of daily changes in the market value of a portfolio that consists of ordinary variable-yield stocks of approximately 40 major Italian companies. It covers mainly manufacturing companies but also includes 14 financial, insurance, and construction companies. Coverage is approximately 60 percent of the total value of stocks admitted to the Milan Exchange.

Exhibit 14-25

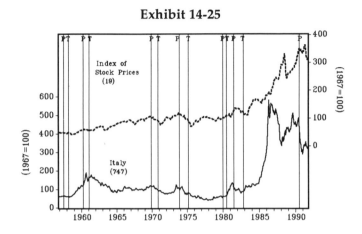

Source: Banca d'Italia (Rome)

JAPAN, Index of Stock Prices (748). This index measures monthly changes in the selling prices of all 690 stocks listed on the Tokyo Exchange. It is compiled with a reference base of April 1, 1968.

Exhibit 14-26

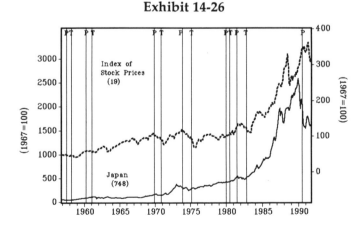

Source: Bank of Japan (Tokyo)

DISCUSSION

With the increased size of the nations (i.e., a unified Germany and a European Common Market), there may be other investment locations for the investor of the future. Investors need two requirements—a large economy and a reliable political climate—before investing in any country. Also many nations are opening stock exchange membership to non-residents and are advocating 24-hour markets.

FOREIGN EXCHANGE RATES

Many times, one has heard that now is the time to travel, or to buy foreign goods. The reason is that, currently, the dollar will buy more foreign currency than at times in the past.

In years past, the gold standard caused exchange rates to fluctuate in a narrow range. This was primarily due to the agreement by the U.S. to buy and sell gold to nations at a fixed rate. Since most currencies were quoted in terms of the amount of gold the nation held, applying the fixed price of gold to the currencies, content became the way to arrive at the approximate rate.

Now, rates are free to fluctuate within ranges set or agreed upon for intervention. At certain points, natural supply of a demand for a particular currency may be manipulated by central banks, activities. The process is not unlike that of a stock manipulator, where the activities were meant to influence stock prices.

Normally, one associates foreign exchange rates with product exports and imports. The effect of fluctuating exchange rates on exports is therefore present. One should remember that capital transfers also have a great deal to do with the demand for the supply of foreign exchange. Capital transfers utilize much greater amounts of foreign exchange than the more often associated exports and imports.

In the graphs, U.S. Exports (602) are shown compared to the national exchange rate per U.S. dollar. On looking at the rates, one should realize that as the dollar can buy more local currency units, imports will be cheaper, but the U.S. exports will be more expensive. The graphs clearly show this relationship, with the effects shown most dramatically in more cases. As the exchange rate of foreign currency per U.S. dollar rises, exports slow down, with resumption noticeable as the dollar becomes more affordable.

Weighted Average Exchange Value of U.S. Dollar Against Currencies of 10 Industrialized Countries (750).

Exhibit 14-27

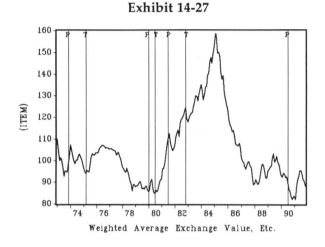

Weighted Average Exchange Value, Etc.

Source: Board of Governors of the Federal Reserve System

Exports (602), Weighted Average (750).

Exhibit 14-28

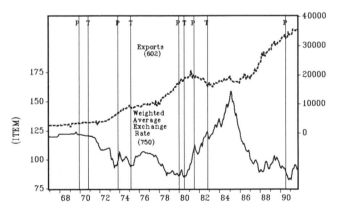

Source: Board of Governors of the Federal Reserve System

CANADA, Exchange Rate Per U.S. Dollar (753).

Exhibit 14-29

Source: Board of Governors of the Federal Reserve System

UNITED KINGDOM, Exchange Rate Per U.S. Dollar (752).

Exhibit 14-30

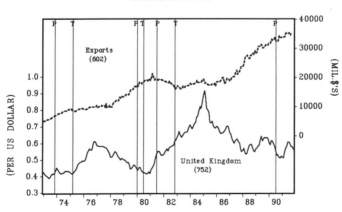

Source: Board of Governors of the Federal Reserve System

FEDERAL REPUBLIC OF GERMANY, Exchange Rate Per U.S. Dollar (755).

Exhibit 14-31

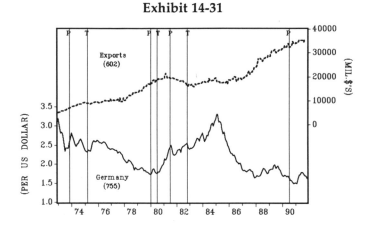

Source: Board of Governors of the Federal Reserve System

FRANCE, Exchange Rate Per U.S. Dollar (756).

Exhibit 14-32

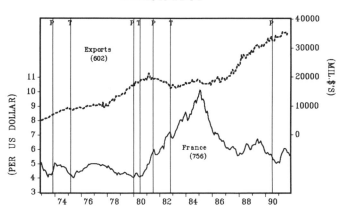

Source: Board of Governors of the Federal Reserve System

ITALY, Exchange Rate Per U.S. Dollar (757).

Exhibit 14-33

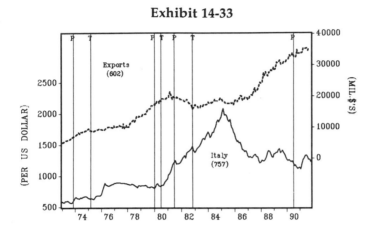

Source: Board of Governors of the Federal Reserve System

JAPAN, Exchange Rate Per U.S. Dollar (758).

Exhibit 14-34

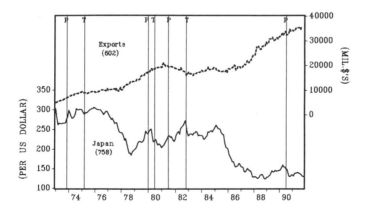

Source: Board of Governors of the Federal Reserve System

DISCUSSION

Fluctuating exchange rates can affect exports dramatically. Even in the U.S., a large percentage change, up or down, results in large changes in exports. At present (1992), the dollar relative to other currencies is low, making the U.S. a favorable place to buy. Hopefully, exports will increase as our rates remain low; but many economies are stretched to a critical point already.

APPENDIX

This diskette series can be received monthly. It includes historical data with start and end dates furnished. Because of the restatements of the NIPA's, the beginning dates of many quarterly series are 1959. Complete restatements will not be available until late 1992.

	BUSINESS CYCLE INDICATORS (BCI) DISKETTE SERIES	
SERIES CODE		**BCI SERIES NUMBER AND TITLE**
A0M001	1.	AVERAGE WEEKLY HOURS, MFG. (HOURS)
LEM001	(1)	CONTRIBUTION OF SERIES 1 TO THE LEADING INDEX
A0M005	5.	AVERAGE WEEKLY INITIAL CLAIMS, UNEMPLOY. INSURANCE (THOUS.)
LEM005	(5)	CONTRIBUTION OF SERIES 5 TO THE LEADING INDEX
A0M007	7.	MFRS' NEW ORDERS, DURABLE GOODS INDUSTRIES (BIL. 1982 $)
A0M008	8.	MFRS' NEW ORDERS, CONSUMER GOODS AND MATERIALS (BIL. 1982 $)
LEM008	(8)	CONTRIBUTION OF SERIES 8 TO THE LEADING INDEX
A0M009	9.	CONSTRUCTION CONTRACTS (MIL. SQ. FT.) COPYRIGHTED (MCGRAW-HILL)
A0M010	10.	CONTRACTS AND ORDERS FOR PLANT AND EQUIPMENT (BIL. $)
A0Q011	11.	NEWLY APPROVED CAPITAL APPROPRIATIONS, MFG. (BIL. $)
A0M012	12.	INDEX OF NET BUSINESS FORMATION (1967=100)
A0M013	13.	NUMBER OF NEW BUSINESS INCORPORATIONS (NUMBER)
U0M014	14.	CURRENT LIABILITIES OF BUSINESS FAILURES, NSA (MIL. $)
A0Q016	16.	CORPORATE PROFITS AFTER TAX (AR, BIL. $)
A0Q018	18.	CORPORATE PROFITS AFTER TAX (AR, BIL. 1987 $)
U0M019	19.	INDEX OF STOCK PRICES, 500 COMMON STOCKS, NSA (1941-43=10)
LEM019	(19)	CONTRIBUTION OF SERIES 19 TO THE LEADING INDEX
F0U019	19.	UNITED STATES, INDEX OF STOCK PRICES, NSA (1967=100)
A0M020	20.	CONTRACTS AND ORDERS FOR PLANT AND EQUIPMENT (BIL. 1982 $)
LEM020	(20)	CONTRIBUTION OF SERIES 20 TO THE LEADING INDEX
A0M021	21.	AVERAGE WEEKLY OVERTIME HOURS, MFG. (HOURS)
A0Q022	22.	RATIO, CORPORATE DOMESTIC PROFITS AFTER TAX TO INCOME (PCT.)
U0M023	23.	SPOT PRICES, RAW MATERIALS, NSA (1967=100) COPYRIGHTED CRB)
A0Q026	26.	RATIO, PRICE TO UNIT LABOR COST, NONFARM BUS. (1982=100)
A0M027	27.	MFRS' NEW ORDERS, NONDEFENSE CAPITAL GOODS (BIL. 1982 $)
A0M028	28.	NEW PRIVATE HOUSING UNITS STARTED (AR, THOUS.)

A0M029	29.	BUILDING PERMITS FOR NEW PRIVATE HOUSING UNITS (1967=100)
LEM029	(29)	CONTRIBUTION OF SERIES 29 TO THE LEADING INDEX
A0Q030	30.	CHANGE IN BUSINESS INVENTORIES (AR, BIL. 1987 $)
A0M031	31.	CHANGE IN MANUFACTURING AND TRADE INVENTORIES (AR, BIL. $)
A0M032	32.	VENDOR PERFORMANCE, SLOWER DELIVERIES DIFFUSION INDEX (PCT.)
LEM032	(32)	CONTRIBUTION OF SERIES 32 TO THE LEADING INDEX
A0Q035	35.	CORPORATE NET CASH FLOW (AR, BIL. 1987 $)
A0M037	37.	NUMBER OF PERSONS UNEMPLOYED (THOUS.)
A0M039	39.	CONSUMER INSTALLMENT LOANS DELINQUENT 30 DAYS & OVER (PCT.)
A0M040	40.	NONAG. EMPLOYEES, GOODS-PRODUCING INDUSTRIES (THOUS.)
A0M041	41.	EMPLOYEES ON NONAGRICULTURAL PAYROLLS (THOUS.)
COM041	(41)	CONTRIBUTION OF SERIES 41 TO THE COINCIDENT INDEX
A0M042	42.	PERSONS ENGAGED IN NONAGRICULTURAL ACTIVITIES (THOUS.)
A0M043	43.	CIVILIAN UNEMPLOYMENT RATE (PCT.)
A0M044	44.	UNEMPLOYMENT RATE, 15 WEEKS AND OVER (PCT.)
A0M045	45.	AVERAGE WEEKLY INSURED UNEMPLOYMENT RATE (PCT.)
A0M046	46.	INDEX OF HELP-WANTED ADVERTISING IN NEWSPAPERS (1967=100)
A0M047	47.	INDEX OF INDUSTRIAL PRODUCTION (1987=100)
COM047	(47)	CONTRIBUTION OF SERIES 47 TO THE COINCIDENT INDEX
A0M048	48.	EMPLOYEE HOURS IN NONAG. ESTABLISHMENTS (AR, BIL. HOURS)
A0Q049	49.	VALUE OF GOODS OUTPUT (AR, BIL. 1987 $)
A0Q050	50.	GROSS NATIONAL PRODUCT (AR, BIL. 1987 $)
P1Q050	50C.	QUARTERLY CHANGE IN GNP IN 1987 $ (AR, PCT.)
A0M051	51.	PERSONAL INCOME LESS TRANSFER PAYMENTS (AR, BIL. 1987 $)
COM051	(51)	CONTRIBUTION OF SERIES 51 TO THE COINCIDENT INDEX
A0M052	52.	PERSONAL INCOME (AR, BIL. 1987 $)
A0M053	53.	WAGES & SALARIES IN MINING, MFG., CONSTR. (AR, BIL. 1982 $)
A0M057	57.	MANUFACTURING AND TRADE SALES (MIL. 1982 $)
COM057	(57)	CONTRIBUTION OF SERIES 57 TO THE COINCIDENT INDEX
U0M058	58.	CONSUMER SENTIMENT, NSA (1966:I=100) COPYRIGHTED (U-MICH)
A0M059	59.	SALES OF RETAIL STORES (MIL. 1982 $)
A0M060	60.	RATIO, HELP-WANTED ADVERTISING TO NUMBER UNEMPLOYED (RATIO)
A0Q061	61.	NEW PLANT & EQUIPMENT EXPENDITURES BY BUSINESS (AR, BIL. $)
A0M062	62A.	INDEX OF LABOR COST PER UNIT OF OUTPUT, MFG. (1987=100)
P1M062	62B.	CHANGE IN LABOR COST PER UNIT OF OUTPUT, MFG. (PCT.)
FLM062	62.	SMOOTHED CHANGE IN LABOR COST PER UNIT OF OUTPUT, MFG. (PCT.)
LGM062	(62)	CONTRIBUTION OF SERIES 62 TO THE LAGGING INDEX
A0Q063	63.	UNIT LABOR COST, ALL PERSONS, BUSINESS SECTOR (1982=100)
A0M066	66.	CONSUMER INSTALLMENT CREDIT OUTSTANDING (MIL. $)
A0M069	69.	MFRS' MACH. & EQUIP. SALES + BUS. CONSTR. EXP. (AR, BIL. $)
A0M070	70.	MANUFACTURING AND TRADE INVENTORIES (BIL. 1982 $)
A0M072	72.	COMMERCIAL AND INDUSTRIAL LOANS OUTSTANDING (MIL. $)
A0M073	73.	INDUSTRIAL PRODUCTION, DURABLE MANUFACTURES (1987=100)
A0M074	74.	INDUSTRIAL PRODUCTION, NONDURABLE MANUFACTURES (1987=100)
A0M075	75.	INDUSTRIAL PRODUCTION, CONSUMER GOODS (1987=100)
A0M076	76.	INDUSTRIAL PRODUCTION, BUSINESS EQUIPMENT (1987=100)
A0M077	77.	RATIO, MFG. AND TRADE INVENTORIES TO SALES IN 1982 $ (RATIO)
LGM077	(77)	CONTRIBUTION OF SERIES 77 TO THE LAGGING INDEX

A0Q081	81.	CORP. DOMESTIC PROFITS WITH IVA & CCADJ TO INCOME (PCT.)
A0M082	82.	CAPACITY UTILIZATION RATE, MANUFACTURING (PCT.)
LEM083	(83)	CONTRIBUTION OF SERIES 83 TO THE LEADING INDEX
U0M083	83.	CONSUMER EXPECTATIONS, NSA (1966:I=100)COPYRIGHTED(U-MICH)
A0M085	85.	CHANGE IN MONEY SUPPLY M1 (PCT.)
A0Q086	86.	NONRESIDENTIAL FIXED INVESTMENT (AR, BIL. 1987 $)
A0Q087	87.	NONRES. FIXED INVESTMENT, STRUCTURES (AR, BIL. 1987 $)
A0Q088	88.	NONRES. FIXED INVEST., PROD. DUR. EQUIP. (AR, BIL. 1987 $)
A0Q089	89.	RESIDENTIAL FIXED INVESTMENT (AR, BIL. 1987 $)
A0M090	90.	RATIO, CIVILIAN EMPLOYMENT TO WORKING-AGE POPULATION (PCT.)
A0M091	91.	AVERAGE DURATION OF UNEMPLOYMENT IN WEEKS (WEEKS)
LGM091	(91)	CONTRIBUTION OF SERIES 91 TO THE LAGGING INDEX
A0M092	92B.	CHANGE IN MFRS' UNFILLED ORDERS, DURABLES (BIL. 1982 $)
A1M092	92A.	MFRS' UNFILLED ORDERS, DURABLE GOODS INDUS. (BIL. 1982 $)
FLM092	92.	SMOOTHED CHANGE IN MFRS' UNFILLED ORDERS (BIL. 1982 $)
LEM092	(92)	CONTRIBUTION OF SERIES 92 TO THE LEADING INDEX
U0M093	93.	FREE RESERVES, NSA (MIL. $)
U0M094	94.	MEMBER BANK BORROWINGS FROM FEDERAL RESERVE, NSA (MIL. $)
A0M095	95.	RATIO, CONSUMER INSTALLMENT CREDIT TO PERSONAL INCOME (PCT.)
LGM095	(95)	CONTRIBUTION OF SERIES 95 TO THE LAGGING INDEX
A0Q097	97.	BACKLOG OF CAPITAL APPROPRIATIONS, MFG. (BIL. $)
A0M098	98.	PRODUCER PRICES—SENS. CRUDE & INTERMED. MTRLS. (1982=100)
A0M099	99B.	CHANGE IN SENSITIVE MATERIALS PRICES (PCT.)
A8M099	99A.	INDEX OF SENSITIVE MATERIALS PRICES (1982=100)
FLM099	99.	SMOOTHED CHANGE IN SENSITIVE MATERIALS PRICES (PCT.)
LEM099	(99)	CONTRIBUTION OF SERIES 99 TO THE LEADING INDEX
A0Q100	100.	NEW PLANT & EQUIPMENT EXPEND. BY BUSINESS (AR, BIL. 1987 $)
A0M101	101.	COMMERCIAL AND INDUSTRIAL LOANS OUTSTANDING (MIL. 1982 $)
LGM101	(101)	CONTRIBUTION OF SERIES 101 TO THE LAGGING INDEX
A0M102	102.	CHANGE IN MONEY SUPPLY M2 (PCT.)
A0M105	105.	MONEY SUPPLY M1 (BIL. 1982 $)
A0M106	106.	MONEY SUPPLY M2 (BIL. 1982 $)
LEM106	(106)	CONTRIBUTION OF SERIES 106 TO THE LEADING INDEX
A0Q107	107.	RATIO, GROSS NATIONAL PRODUCT TO MONEY SUPPLY M1 (RATIO)
A0M108	108.	RATIO, PERSONAL INCOME TO MONEY SUPPLY M2 (RATIO)
U0M109	109.	AVERAGE PRIME RATE CHARGED BY BANKS, NSA (PCT.)
LGM109	(109)	CONTRIBUTION OF SERIES 109 TO THE LAGGING INDEX
A0Q110	110.	FUNDS RAISED BY PRIVATE NONFINANCIAL BORROWERS (AR, MIL. $)
A0M111	111.	CHANGE IN BUSINESS AND CONSUMER CREDIT (AR, PCT.)
A0M112	112.	NET CHANGE IN BUSINESS LOANS (AR, BIL. $)
A0M113	113.	NET CHANGE IN CONSUMER INSTALLMENT CREDIT (AR, BIL. $)
U0M114	114.	DISCOUNT RATE ON NEW 91-DAY TREASURY BILLS, NSA (PCT.)
U0M115	115.	YIELD ON LONG-TERM TREASURY BONDS, NSA (PCT.)
U0M116	120.	SMOOTHED CHANGE IN CPI FOR SERVICES (AR, PCT.)
LGM120	(120)	CONTRIBUTION OF SERIES 120 TO THE LAGGING INDEX
A0M120	120B.	CHANGE IN CPI FOR SERVICES (AR, PCT.)
A8M120	120A.	CONSUMER PRICE INDEX FOR SERVICES (1982-84=100)
A0M122	122.	INDEX OF CONSUMER CONFIDENCE (1985=100)

A0M123   123.   INDEX OF CONSUMER EXPECTATIONS (1985=100)
A0M124   124.   CAPACITY UTILIZATION RATE, TOTAL INDUSTRY (PCT.)
A0Q290   290.   GROSS SAVING (AR, BIL. $)
A0Q292   292.   PERSONAL SAVING (AR, BIL. $)
A0Q293   293.   PERSONAL SAVING RATE (PCT.)
A0Q295   295.   BUSINESS SAVING (AR, BIL. $)
A0Q298   298.   GOVERNMENT SURPLUS OR DEFICIT (AR, BIL. $)
A0Q310   310.   IMPLICIT PRICE DEFLATOR FOR GNP (1982=100)
P1Q310   310C.   CHANGE IN GNP IMPLICIT PRICE DEFLATOR (AR, PCT.)
A0Q311   311.   FIXED-WTD. PRICE INDEX, GROSS DOM. BUS. PRODUCT (1982=100)
P1Q311   311C.   CHANGE IN FIXED-WTD. PRICE INDEX, GDBP (AR, PCT.)
U0M320   320.   CPI FOR ALL URBAN CONSUMERS, ALL ITEMS, NSA (1982-84=100)
P1M320   320C.   CHANGE IN CPI-U, ALL ITEMS, 1-MONTH SPAN (PCT.)
P6M320   320C.   CHANGE IN CPI-U, ALL ITEMS, 6-MONTH SPAN (AR, PCT.)
A0M323   323.   CPI-U, ALL ITEMS LESS FOOD AND ENERGY (1982-84=100)
P1M323   323C.   CHANGE IN CPI-U, LESS FOOD & ENERGY, 1-MO. SPAN (PCT.)
P6M323   323C.   CHANGE IN CPI-U, LESS FOOD & ENERGY, 6-MO. SPAN (AR, PCT.)
A0M331   331.   PRODUCER PRICE INDEX, CRUDE MATERIALS (1982=100)
P1M331   331C.   CHANGE IN PPI, CRUDE MATERIALS, 1-MONTH SPAN (PCT.)
P6M331   331C.   CHANGE IN PPI, CRUDE MATERIALS, 6-MONTH SPAN (AR, PCT.)
A0M332   332.   PRODUCER PRICE INDEX, INTERMEDIATE MATERIALS (1982=100)
P1M332   332C.   CHANGE IN PPI, INTERMEDIATE MATERIALS, 1-MO. SPAN (PCT.)
P6M332   332C.   CHANGE IN PPI, INTERMED. MATERIALS, 6-MO. SPAN (AR, PCT.)
A0M333   333.   PRODUCER PRICE INDEX, CAPITAL EQUIPMENT (1982=100)
P1M333   333C.   CHANGE IN PPI, CAPITAL EQUIPMENT, 1-MONTH SPAN (PCT.)
P6M333   333C.   CHANGE IN PPI, CAPITAL EQUIPMENT, 6-MONTH SPAN (AR, PCT.)
A0M334   334.   PRODUCER PRICE INDEX, FINISHED CONSUMER GOODS (1982=100)
P1M334   334C.   CHANGE IN PPI, FINISHED CONSUMER GOODS, 1-MO. SPAN (PCT.)
P6M334   334C.   CHANGE IN PPI, FINISHED CONS. GOODS, 6-MO. SPAN (AR, PCT.)
A0M336   336.   PRODUCER PRICE INDEX, FINISHED GOODS (1982=100)
P1M336   336C.   CHANGE IN PPI, FINISHED GOODS, 1-MONTH SPAN (PCT.)
P6M336   336C.   CHANGE IN PPI, FINISHED GOODS, 6-MONTH SPAN (AR, PCT.)
A0M337   337.   PPI, FINISHED GOODS LESS FOODS AND ENERGY (1982=100)
P1M337   337C.   CHANGE IN PPI, LESS FOODS & ENERGY, 1-MO. SPAN (PCT.)
P6M337   337C.   CHANGE IN PPI, LESS FOODS & ENERGY, 6-MO. SPAN (AR, PCT.)
A0Q345   345.   AVERAGE HOURLY COMPENSATION, NONFARM BUS. SECTOR (1982=100)
P1Q345   345C.   CHANGE IN AVG. HOURLY COMPENSATION (AR, PCT.)
A0Q346   346.   REAL AVG. HOURLY COMPENSATION, NONFARM BUSINESS (1982=100)
P1Q346   346C.   CHANGE IN REAL AVG. HOURLY COMPENSATION (AR, PCT.)
A0Q358   358.   OUTPUT PER HOUR, NONFARM BUSINESS SECTOR (1982=100)
A0Q370   370.   OUTPUT PER HOUR, BUSINESS SECTOR (1982=100)
P1Q370   370C.   CHANGE IN OUTPUT PER HOUR, 1-Q SPAN (AR, PCT.)
P4Q370   370C.   CHANGE IN OUTPUT PER HOUR, 4-Q SPAN (AR, PCT.)
A0M441   441.   CIVILIAN LABOR FORCE (THOUS.)
A0M442   442.   CIVILIAN EMPLOYMENT (THOUS.)
A0M451   451.   LABOR FORCE PARTICIPATION RATE, MALES 20 AND OVER (PCT.)
A0M452   452.   LABOR FORCE PARTICIPATION RATE, FEMALES 20 AND OVER (PCT.)
A0M453   453.   LABOR FORCE PARTICIPATION RATE, 16-19 YEARS OF AGE (PCT.)

A0M517	517.	DEFENSE DEPARTMENT GROSS OBLIGATIONS INCURRED (MIL. $)
A0M525	525.	DEFENSE DEPARTMENT PRIME CONTRACT AWARDS IN U.S. (MIL. $)
A0M543	543.	DEFENSE DEPT. GROSS UNPAID OBLIGATIONS OUTSTANDING (MIL. $)
A0M548	548.	MANUFACTURERS' NEW ORDERS, DEFENSE PRODUCTS (MIL. $)
A0M557	557.	INDUSTRIAL PRODUCTION, DEFENSE & SPACE EQUIPMENT (1987=100)
A0Q564	564.	FEDERAL GOVERNMENT PURCHASES, NATIONAL DEFENSE (AR, BIL. $)
A0M570	570.	EMPLOYMENT, DEFENSE PRODUCTS INDUSTRIES (THOUS.)
A0M602	602.	EXPORTS, EXCLUDING MILITARY AID SHIPMENTS (MIL. $)
A0M604	604.	EXPORTS OF DOMESTIC AGRICULTURAL PRODUCTS (MIL. $)
A0M606	606.	EXPORTS OF NONELECTRICAL MACHINERY (MIL. $)
A0M612	612.	GENERAL IMPORTS (MIL. $)
A0M614	614.	IMPORTS OF PETROLEUM AND PETROLEUM PRODUCTS (MIL. $)
A0M616	616.	IMPORTS OF AUTOMOBILES AND PARTS (MIL. $)
A0Q618	618.	MERCHANDISE EXPORTS, ADJUSTED, EXCLUDING MILITARY (MIL. $)
A0Q620	620.	MERCHANDISE IMPORTS, ADJUSTED, EXCLUDING MILITARY (MIL. $)
A0Q622	622.	BALANCE ON MERCHANDISE TRADE (MIL. $)
A0M721	721.	OECD, EUROPEAN COUNTRIES, INDUSTRIAL PRODUCTION (1987=100)
A0M722	722.	UNITED KINGDOM, INDUSTRIAL PRODUCTION (1987=100)
A0M723	723.	CANADA, INDUSTRIAL PRODUCTION (1987=100)
A0M725	725.	FED. REPUBLIC OF GERMANY, INDUSTRIAL PRODUCTION (1987=100)
A0M726	726.	FRANCE, INDUSTRIAL PRODUCTION (1987=100)
A0M727	727.	ITALY, INDUSTRIAL PRODUCTION (1987=100)
A0M728	728.	JAPAN, INDUSTRIAL PRODUCTION (1987=100)
U0M732	732.	UNITED KINGDOM, CONSUMER PRICE INDEX, NSA (1982-84=100)
P6M732	732C.	UNITED KINGDOM, 6-MO. CHANGE IN CONSUMER PRICES (AR, PCT.)
U0M733	733.	CANADA, CONSUMER PRICE INDEX, NSA (1982-84=100)
P6M733	733C.	CANADA, 6-MONTH CHANGE IN CONSUMER PRICES (AR, PCT.)
U0M735	735.	GERMANY, CONSUMER PRICE INDEX, NSA (1982-84=100)
P6M735	735C.	GERMANY, 6-MONTH CHANGE IN CONSUMER PRICES (AR, PCT.)
U0M736	736.	FRANCE, CONSUMER PRICE INDEX, NSA (1982-84=100)
P6M736	736C.	FRANCE, 6-MONTH CHANGE IN CONSUMER PRICES (AR, PCT.)
U0M737	737.	ITALY, CONSUMER PRICE INDEX, NSA (1982-84=100)
P6M737	737C.	ITALY, 6-MONTH CHANGE IN CONSUMER PRICES (AR, PCT.)
U0M738	738.	JAPAN, CONSUMER PRICE INDEX, NSA (1982-84=100)
P6M738	738C.	JAPAN, 6-MONTH CHANGE IN CONSUMER PRICES (AR, PCT.)
U0M742	742.	UNITED KINGDOM, STOCK PRICES, NSA (1967=100)
U0M743	743.	CANADA, STOCK PRICES, NSA (1967=100)
U0M745	745.	FEDERAL REPUBLIC OF GERMANY, STOCK PRICES, NSA (1967=100)
U0M746	746.	FRANCE, STOCK PRICES, NSA (1967=100)
U0M747	747.	ITALY, STOCK PRICES, NSA (1967=100)
U0M748	748.	JAPAN, STOCK PRICES, NSA (1967=100)
U0M750	750.	EXCHANGE VALUE OF U.S. DOLLAR, NSA (MAR. 1973=100)
U0M752	752.	UNITED KINGDOM, EXCHANGE RATE PER U.S. DOLLAR, NSA (POUND)
U0M753	753.	CANADA, EXCHANGE RATE PER U.S. DOLLAR, NSA (DOLLAR)
U0M755	755.	GERMANY, EXCHANGE RATE PER U.S. DOLLAR, NSA (D. MARK)
U0M756	756.	FRANCE, EXCHANGE RATE PER U.S. DOLLAR, NSA (FRANC)
U0M757	757.	ITALY, EXCHANGE RATE PER U.S. DOLLAR, NSA (LIRA)
U0M758	758.	JAPAN, EXCHANGE RATE PER U.S. DOLLAR, NSA (YEN)

G0M910	910.	COMPOSITE INDEX OF 11 LEADING INDICATORS (1982=100)
PCM910	910C.	LEADING INDEX, CHANGE FROM PREVIOUS MONTH (PCT.)
P1M910	910C.	LEADING INDEX, CHANGE OVER 1-MONTH SPAN (AR, PCT.)
P3M910	910C.	LEADING INDEX, CHANGE OVER 3-MONTH SPAN (AR, PCT.)
G0M920	920.	COMPOSITE INDEX OF 4 COINCIDENT INDICATORS (1982=100)
PCM920	920C.	COINCIDENT INDEX, CHANGE FROM PREVIOUS MONTH (PCT.)
P1M920	920C.	COINCIDENT INDEX, CHANGE OVER 1-MONTH SPAN (AR, PCT.)
P3M920	920C.	COINCIDENT INDEX, CHANGE OVER 3-MONTH SPAN (AR, PCT.)
G0M930	930.	COMPOSITE INDEX OF 7 LAGGING INDICATORS (1982=100)
PCM930	930C.	LAGGING INDEX, CHANGE FROM PREVIOUS MONTH (PCT.)
P1M930	930C.	LAGGING INDEX, CHANGE OVER 1-MONTH SPAN (AR, PCT.)
P3M930	930C.	LAGGING INDEX, CHANGE OVER 3-MONTH SPAN (AR, PCT.)
G0M940	940.	RATIO, COINCIDENT INDEX TO LAGGING INDEX (1982=100)
D1M950	950.	DIFFUSION INDEX OF LEADING INDICATORS, 1-MO. SPAN (PCT.)
D6M950	950.	DIFFUSION INDEX OF LEADING INDICATORS, 6-MO. SPAN (PCT.)
D1M951	951.	DIFFUSION INDEX OF COINCIDENT INDICATORS, 1-MO. SPAN (PCT.)
D6M951	951.	DIFFUSION INDEX OF COINCIDENT INDICATORS, 6-MO. SPAN (PCT.)
D1M952	952.	DIFFUSION INDEX OF LAGGING INDICATORS, 1-MO. SPAN (PCT.)
D6M952	952.	DIFFUSION INDEX OF LAGGING INDICATORS, 6-MO. SPAN (PCT.)
D1M963	963.	PRIVATE NONAG. EMPLOYMENT, 1-MO. DIFFUSION INDEX (PCT.)
D6M963	963.	PRIVATE NONAG. EMPLOYMENT, 6-MO. DIFFUSION INDEX (PCT.)
SAM411	(98)	PRODUCER PRICE INDEX, CATTLE HIDES (1982=100)
X9MP08	(98)	PRODUCER PRICE INDEX, LUMBER AND WOOD PRODUCTS (1982=100)
S2M102	(98)	PRODUCER PRICE INDEX, WASTEPAPER, NEWS (1982=100)
N2M205	(98)	PRODUCER PRICE INDEX, WASTEPAPER, MIXED, NSA (1982=100)
S2M311	(98)	PRODUCER PRICE INDEX, WASTEPAPER, CORRUGATED (1982=100)
SAM012	(98)	PRODUCER PRICE INDEX, IRON AND STEEL SCRAP (1982=100)
PPMCOP	(98)	PRODUCER PRICE INDEX, COPPER BASE SCRAP (1982=100)
PPMALM0	(98)	PRODUCER PRICE INDEX, ALUMINUM BASE SCRAP (1982=100)
T0M303	(98)	PRODUCER PRICE INDEX, NONFERROUS SCRAP, NSA (1982=100)
SAM892	(98)	PRODUCER PRICE INDEX, SAND, GRAVEL, AND STONE (1982=100)
S3MCAS	(98)	PRODUCER PRICE INDEX, RAW COTTON (1982=100)
S4MCAS	(98)	PRODUCER PRICE INDEX, DOMESTIC APPAREL WOOL (1982=100)
S1M967	(23)	SPOT PRICE, COPPER SCRAP ($ PER LB.) COPYRIGHTED (CRB)
S2M967	(23)	SPOT PRICE, LEAD SCRAP ($ PER LB.) COPYRIGHTED (CRB)
S3M967	(23)	SPOT PRICE, STEEL SCRAP ($ PER TON) COPYRIGHTED (CRB)
Y4M967	(23)	SPOT PRICE, TIN, NSA ($ PER LB.) COPYRIGHTED (CRB)
Y5M967	(23)	SPOT PRICE, ZINC, NSA ($ PER LB.) COPYRIGHTED (CRB)
Y6M967	(23)	SPOT PRICE, BURLAP, NSA ($ PER YD.) COPYRIGHTED (CRB)
S7M967	(23)	SPOT PRICE, COTTON ($ PER LB.) COPYRIGHTED (CRB)
Y8M967	(23)	SPOT PRICE, PRINT CLOTH, NSA ($ PER YD.) COPYRIGHTED (CRB)
Y9M967	(23)	SPOT PRICE, WOOL TOPS, NSA ($ PER LB.) COPYRIGHTED (CRB)
Y1M067	(23)	SPOT PRICE, HIDES, NSA ($ PER LB.) COPYRIGHTED (CRB)
S1M167	(23)	SPOT PRICE, ROSIN ($ PER 100 LB.) COPYRIGHTED (CRB)
S1M267	(23)	SPOT PRICE, RUBBER ($ PER LB.) COPYRIGHTED (CRB)
S1M367	(23)	SPOT PRICE, TALLOW ($ PER LB.) COPYRIGHTED (CRB)
G0M990	990.	CIBCR LONG-LEADING COMPOSITE INDEX (1967=100)
G0M991	991.	CIBCR SHORT-LEADING COMPOSITE INDEX (1967=100)

REFERENCES CITED

Billingsley, Patrick, D. James Croft, David V. Huntsberger, Collin J. Watson. *Statistical Inference for Management and Economics*. pp. 557-558. Boston: Allyn and Bacon, Inc., 1986.

Burns, Arthur F., and Wesley C. Mitchell. *Measuring Business Cycles*. New York: National Bureau of Economic Research, 1946.

Council of Economic Advisors. *Economic Indicators*. Washington, D.C.: GPO, 1990.

Dubois, Edward N. *Essential Statistical Methods for Business*. pp. 273-274. New York: McGraw-Hill, Inc., 1979.

Fabozzi, Frank J., and Harry I. Greenfield eds. *The Handbook of Economic and Financial Measures*. Homewood, IL: Dow Jones - Irwin, 1984.

Fels, Rindigs, and C. Elton Hinshaw. *Forecasting and Recognizing Business Cycle Turning Points*. New York: National Bureau of Economic Research, 1968.

Financial Accounting Standards Board. *Quantitative Characteristics of Accounting Information*. Statement No. 2. Stamford, CN: FASB, 1980.

Gordon, Robert J., ed. *The American Business Cycle*. Chicago: The University of Chicago Press, 1986.

Hertzberg, Marie P., and Berry A. Beckman. Business cycle indicators: revised composite indexes. *Business Conditions Digest*. January, 1989, pp. 97-102. U.S. Department of Commerce, Bureau of Economic Analysis, Washington, D.C.: GPO.

Johnston, J. *Economic Methods*. New York: Mc Graw-Hill, 1984.

Mitchell, Wesley Clair. *Business Cycles and Their Causes*. Berkeley, CA: University of California Press, 1960.

Moore, Geoffrey H., ed. *Business Cycle Indicators*. National Bureau of Economic Research, Volume I. Princeton, NJ: Princeton University Press, 1961.

_____. *Leading Indicators for the 1990s*. Homewood, IL: Dow Jones-Irwin, 1990.

Moore, Geoffrey H., and Melita H. Moore. *International Economic Indicators*. Westport, CN: Greenwood Press, 1985.

Moore, Geoffrey H., and Julius Shiskin. *Indicators of Business Expansions and Contractions*. New York: National Bureau of Economic Research, 1967.

National Bureau of Economic Research. Business cycle expansions and contractions in the United States. *Business Conditions Digest*. January, 1990, p. 104. U.S. Department of Commerce, Bureau of Economic Analysis, Washington, D.C.: GPO.

Parker, Robert P. A preview of the comprehensive revision of the national income and product accounts, definitional and classificational changes. *Business Conditions Digest*. September, 1991, pp. 23-25, 30 and 31. U. S. Department of Commerce Bureau of Economic Analysis, Washington, D.C.: GPO.

Pindyck, Roberts S., and Daniel L. Rubinefild. *Econometric Models and Economic Forecasts*, 3rd ed. New York: McGraw-Hill, 1990.

U.S. Department of Commerce, Bureau of the Census. *Statistical Abstract of the United States*, 11th ed. Washington, D.C.: GPO, 1990.

U.S. Department of Commerce, Bureau of Economic Analysis. *Handbook of Cyclical Indicators*. Washington, D.C.: GPO, 1977.

——————————. Bureau of Economic Analysis. *Handbook of Cyclical Indicators*. Washington, D.C.: GPO, 1984.

Zarnowitz, Victor, and Charlotte Boschan. Cyclical indicators: an evaluation and new leading indicators. *Handbook of Cyclical Indicators*. (pp. 170-184) U.S. Department of Commerce, Bureau of Economic Analysis. Washington, D.C.: GPO, 1977.

Zarnowitz, Victor, and Charlotte Boschan. New composite indexes of coincident and lagging indicators. *Handbook of Cyclical Indicators*. (pp. 185-198) U.S. Department of Commerce, Bureau of Economic Analysis. Washington, D.C.: GPO, 1977.

Zarnowitz, Victor, and Geoffrey Moore. "Major Changes in Cyclical Behavior." *The American Business Cycle*, Robert J. Gordon, ed., pp. 519-582. Chicago: University of Chicago Press, 1986.

SERIES NUMBER INDEX

ALPHABETIC INDEX